JULIE TAYMOR
PLAYING WITH FIRE

JULIE TAYMOR
PLAYING WITH FIRE

Theater

Opera

Film

Eileen Blumenthal • Julie Taymor

HARRY N. ABRAMS, INC., PUBLISHERS

EDITOR: Diana Murphy
DESIGNER: Maria Learmonth Miller
PHOTO EDITOR: John K. Crowley

FRONTISPIECE: Julie Taymor with her masks from *Juan Darién*
Photograph by Josef Astor

LIBRARY OF CONGRESS CATALOGING—IN—PUBLICATION DATA

Blumenthal, Eileen, 1948–
Julie Taymor, playing with fire : theater, opera, film / Eileen
    Blumenthal, Julie Taymor.
p.   cm.
Includes index.
ISBN 0–8109–3879–0
1. Taymor, Julie, 1952–   —Criticism and interpretation.
2. Experimental theater.   I. Taymor, Julie, 1952–   . II. Title.
PN2287.T28B58   1995
792'.0233'092—dc20
                                                                94–48321

Published in 1995 by Harry N. Abrams, Incorporated, New York
A Times Mirror Company
All rights reserved. No part of the contents of this book
may be reproduced without the written permission of the publisher

Printed and bound in Japan

CONTENTS

JULIE TAYMOR

Eileen Blumenthal

Her cheeks and breasts distressed as if from years of sea winds, a giant figurehead labeled "The Havoc" greets visitors to Julie Taymor's New York apartment. Past this veteran of *Liberty's Taken*, Taymor's musical about the American Revolution, a dozen white doors line a living-room wall, like the setting for a Meyerhold farce. Indonesian batik and *ikat* weavings cover a sofa. Nearby, two-foot-high Javanese peasants, which Taymor carved for *Way of Snow*, peer out between philodendron leaves, and tiny mask-totems adorned with chicken feathers, from the same show, rest on a window sill. A ten-foot-long, bas-relief Brazilian Indian from Taymor's design for *Savages* nurses her baby in a jute hammock overhead. A sharp-planed, alabaster bust from *Juan Darién* casts a critical eye around the room from his perch atop a stool. And somehow it all blends to evoke a sense of elegance and home.

The design of Taymor's loft hints at the nature of her genius—why, in less than two decades since she cut her theatrical teeth in Indonesia, she has developed into one of our most accomplished directors—one Harold Prince has described as blessed with a "rare visionary gift."[1]

Taymor's work—in theater, opera, and film—is not so much eclectic as it is cross-bred. She draws on an enormous pool of forms, genres, traditions. She grasps the center of each form, how it works in its home context and how it might resonate somewhere else. She conceives new theatrical organisms, combining traits from the most disparate sources to bring original hybrids to life.

This wild cross-pollinating spans cultures—but Taymor the genetic engineer works in the service of Taymor the director. In *The Transposed Heads*, her adaptation of a German novella set in India, she draws on traditions as diverse as eighteenth-century Japanese puppetry and modern performance-art. But each technique directly underscores elements of plot or theme. The gaunt, blue Bunraku puppet she designed to play an old ascetic seems removed from everyday life, as he should be, and can levitate on cue. By projecting fluid, abstract images onto moving layers of scrim, Taymor creates a setting of hologramlike shimmers, perfect for a play about the evanescence of identity and reality.

Usually she assimilates disparate elements rather than leaving them in native dress. Only historians of European theater might notice how closely the stage arrangement in Taymor's design for a Passover *Haggadah* pageant resembles that of medieval Christian Passion plays. Only viewers familiar with Chinese theater would be likely to realize that the show's Red Sea of billowing cloth derives from a Peking Opera convention. Taymor's *Juan Darién* incorporates techniques from Japan, Indonesia, Czechoslovakia, and Western

"The Havoc," a ship's figurehead from Liberty's Taken.

OPPOSITE: *The mother's room and images of mourning in* Juan Darién.

The Bunraku-technique ascetic, Kamadamana, in The Transposed Heads, *executes an ecstatic grand battement.*

fairgrounds, as well as pure products of Taymor's imagination. But they meld into one coherent presentation of a South American village.

Taymor culls elements from across theatrical genres as well as national boundaries. Her direction of Stravinsky's *Oedipus Rex* in Japan respects the integrity of the music (conducted by Seiji Ozawa and sung by Jessye Norman, Philip Langridge, and Bryn Terfel). But she double-casts Oedipus with a silent alter-ego, a Japanese avant-garde Butoh dancer. In *Juan Darién*, Taymor and her longtime collaborator Elliot Goldenthal counterpoint a through-sung score of operatic, ecclesiastical density with slapstick hand-puppetry and raunchy, scatological shadow plays.

One of Taymor's most interesting cross-breedings is between film and stage. Her theater often manipulates scale and viewing angles to achieve such filmic effects as pans, zooms, and close-ups. In *Juan Darién*, a funeral procession of tiny puppets makes its way along the miniature paths of a ten-foot-high mountain village—creating the live equivalent of a wide-angle shot. Meanwhile, giant images of mourning and prayer appear around the stage: two women kneeling over a corpse, an oversized mask of a head and two supplicating hands —in effect, mid-range and close-up shots. Gradually, lights come on in the tiny houses one by one—like a camera tracking through the village—and the audience sees shadow-puppet silhouettes of the life inside: a woman combs a girl's hair; a couple makes love; another fights violently; a woman cradles her baby. Then, the whole village rotates. As if a camera has zoomed in, the reverse side of the mound contains in human scale the room of the woman rocking what the audience now sees is a tiny coffin.

Conversely, Taymor translates the most characteristic effects of live theater—such as curtains rising—onto film. *Fool's Fire*, her adaptation of Edgar Allan Poe's "Hop-Frog," opens with a close-up of a red cabbage leaf. Gradually a rat nibbles it away, revealing the scene behind it, a family of dwarfs at dinner. The sinister rat image clashes perfectly with the sense of expectation the disappearing leaf creates of an Act I curtain going up. In fact, Taymor often simply straddles film and theater by using shadow puppetry, which is, in effect, live cinema.

Her work ranges from extravaganzas of ingenious staging to relatively spare mise-en-scènes, depending on the stories and, even more, on the themes. To express extremes of experience, she invents fanciful or grotesque worlds filled with created actors. For work rooted in more conventional human psychology, she develops more familiar universes populated by people. And while she began her career using mainly Asia-derived forms in original creations, over the past decade she has also focused more and more on Western classics.

Taymor's training has included mime, filmmaking, ritual and masked dance, method acting, experimental ensemble creation, and puppetry technique. She has studied or apprenticed not only around the United States but also in Paris and Indonesia. For all this, she has never formally studied art, stage design, or directing. She prefers to start out *not* knowing how things are supposed to be done—and what supposedly cannot be done. She immerses herself in research, formulates a plan, and jumps in. Formally trained mainly as a performer, she has conceived and undertaken ambitious projects in which she has also designed, adapted nontheatrical material, written stage- and screenplays, and directed—in theater, opera, and film.

An omnivorous viewer of the arts, she finds nourishing nuggets in all sorts of places. Among her inspirations have been a one-minute-long puppet play in Holland and a tree festooned with roasted piglets in Bali.

Beginnings

In retrospect, the path that led Julie Taymor from a comfortable Boston suburb to Bali to world opera stages seems as inevitable as it was circuitous. The concerns and passions that have shaped her work trace back in remarkable degree to very early experiences.

*Taymor in Sri Lanka at age fifteen,
looking out at the Indian Ocean.*

Born in 1952, the youngest child of a Democratic activist mother and gynecologist father, Julie Taymor was doing backyard theater by age seven. Her sister organized stagings of children's stories at their house, and Julie not only acted but made the scenery and props.

By the age of ten, Taymor had developed what she even now calls "a real seriousness about theater." She began to attend the Boston Children's Theater, a disciplined, professionally oriented group. She loved both the rigor and the creativity, as BCT nurtured her interest in theater that went beyond the literal and imitative. Exercises like "being frightened with your toes" sparked her imagination. Also, the theater's mixed racial and social population triggered an engagement with diverse cultures that has infused nearly all her work.

Taymor's cross-cultural interests soon turned more global. During high school, she spent a summer traveling in India and Sri Lanka with the Experiment in International Living. She found this first exposure to traditional Asian performance exciting, but the forms too detailed and busy for her taste. What did stun her was the richness and extremity of the street life. For an American teenager, this was an amazingly polychromatic world—where itinerant poets and snake charmers shared the sidewalks with businessmen and women wrapped in luminous silks, and the smells of spices, bus fumes, and humanity mingled.

As she took in the sights, sounds, and odors, Taymor also monitored her reactions. She noted that just two months after their initial shock at seeing street beggars (still at that time uncommon in America), the students were no longer quite so upset by it. This life lesson about how easily people can become anaesthetized to the suffering of others ultimately proved an important insight for directing.

Back in Newton, Massachusetts, in 1969 for her last year of high school, Taymor joined Julie Portman's Theater Workshop of Boston, where, at fifteen, she was the youngest member. Ensemble creation was the avant-garde trend. In 1967–68, Joseph Chaikin's Open Theater had developed *The Serpent*, and other experimental artists were exploring similar routes. Taymor's workshop, run by Barbara Linden, did research and improvisations on Native Americans, developing a piece called *Tribe*, which they performed at a local church.

At this point, Taymor wanted more rigorous physical training. So, after finishing high school a semester early, at age sixteen, she headed for Paris to study at L'École de Mime Jacques LeCoq. She was not interested in mime as a performance goal per se, but in refining her use of the body to convey character and emotion. At LeCoq Taymor began working with masks. Students had to adapt their bodies not only to character masks but to abstract, geometric faces. They also animated objects such as bottles, brooms, and wastebaskets—seeking their inherent character and then physicalizing it, in effect turning them into puppets.

During her year in Paris, Taymor went nearly every day to the Cinémathèque, where she was especially inspired by Fellini and Kurosawa. Without a conscious program, she was learning the art of film—aesthetics and techniques that she would later use not only in her film work but also in live theater.

In 1970, Taymor entered Oberlin College in Ohio. After one year there, she enrolled in a program that allowed her to earn credit away from school, apprenticing with a theater company. So during one of the most fertile periods of off-off-Broadway, Julie Taymor was in residence with Joseph Chaikin's Open Theater, Robert Kalfin's Chelsea Theater Company, and Peter Schumann's Bread and Puppet Theater. Following that semester, she remained in New York for several months. She studied acting at the Herbert Berghof School, made the rounds of auditions, and got some acting work. She also took anthropology courses at Columbia University, including one taught by Margaret Mead.

Meanwhile, news came from Oberlin that the experimental director Herbert Blau would be moving there from California Institute of the Arts to start a professional theater company, bringing along the core of a troupe. Taymor auditioned, and the following fall, she returned to Ohio as the youngest member of Blau's group.

The new company of about fifteen actors worked intensely, often seven hours a day, five days a week. Like many avant-gardists of the time, Blau was inspired by Jerzy Grotowski's model of ferociously rigorous training. Taymor recalls the work as "immensely grueling, both physically and mentally. And challenging."

While much of the avant-garde in this period mistrusted words and ideas, both were integral to Blau's approach. "The conceptualization was so intensely part of what was performed," Blau recalls, "that unless you were prepared to think this way, you couldn't do the work." And though Taymor considered herself at the time to be mainly visually and physically oriented and not especially

Agamemnon (Tyran Russel), Orestes (Bill Irwin), and Electra (Taymor) in The Seeds of Atreus.

intellectual, Blau recalls her as not only "very, very smart" but adventurous, with "a quizzical take on things," raising conceptual as well as theatrical questions. In fact, a strong rooting in ideas as well as emotions and pictures has distinguished all of Taymor's own theater.

During its first year, The Oberlin Group's main project was an ensemble-created theater piece called *The Seeds of Atreus*, based on *The Oresteia*. Blau charged the performers to find "ideographs" of the actions—pared-down forms that contained the essence. In conception, Blau's ideographs were "tightly formed, consolidated, volatile moments of apprehended energy." The ideograph functioned, he says, like a "vortex": "Everything outside it is whirling in a kind of indeterminate way, but as you get toward the center it becomes dense, and it focuses the mind with sufficient intensity that it explodes it outward." In practice, these compact, spare moments helped the director and performers capture and express the kernel of each action without the distracting details. (For example, as the barren Electra, Taymor developed a gesture of slapping her womb and then reaching out as if in supplication.) In this way, the artists could shape the audience's focus. Ideographs not only carried concentrated meaning but also became icons of a sort, a theatrical sign language that facilitated the layering and counterpointing of subtexts. Blau's concept of ideographs, Taymor says, combined with her LeCoq training in precise physical expression, has informed absolutely everything she has done in the theater since then.

For the second season, Blau pared his workshop down to seven actors—including Taymor, Bill Irwin, and David Suehsdorf. The project that year was an ensemble creation about the Donner Party, the 1846 expedition to California that became trapped in a freak snowstorm, and whose survivors lasted partly by cannibalism. Blau's actors improvised scenes based on documentary materials, including letters, journals, and newspaper clippings.

While generating individual segments, they looked for a structure. Taymor suggested contemporary square dance. The action became framed in a night at the dance, with the movements reflecting the dancers' relationships of rivalry, love, hunger. Blau constructed a text relating the Donner Party story, which the company performed within the complicated patterns of the dance. Again, Taymor says, the Blau workshop taught her fundamental lessons about refining a story into its key elements—turning raw material into a play.

In the final version of *The Donner Party*, Taymor played a pioneer, an Indian, an ox, and elements of the landscape. Blau also wrote a long monologue for her unlike anything else in the play, based on a several-hour improvisation she had done. He describes it as "a no-nonsense speech, absolutely modeled on Julie. She talks about the absurdity of the trip, the inadequacy of the people. It's elliptical, but she's obviously talking about our group—this one has a bad attitude, this one's screwing up." It was clear at the outset, Blau says, that while Taymor was cooperative and "very game," she was "very strong-minded." Blau wanted to capture that tenacity in *The Donner Party*. Meanwhile, seeing her words altered by context, Taymor was struck by the power of a director or editor to reinforce or distort material.

Taymor as Tamsen Donner in The Donner Party.

During college, Taymor also did more traditional theater. She designed puppets for a college production of Brecht's *The Elephant Calf* and played Kate in a student production of *The Taming of the Shrew*. And she directed and designed scenes from *Peer Gynt*, experimenting with scale by including shadow-puppet trolls inside the mountain, finger puppets, and actors in giant masks.

Meanwhile, she put together an academic major in folklore and mythology, studying origins of theater in shamanic ritual and totems. In 1973, she attended a summer program of the American Society for Eastern Arts in Seattle. Instructors included performers of Indonesian *topeng* masked dance-drama and *wayang kulit* shadow puppetry, which was Taymor's focus.

After graduating from college (Phi Beta Kappa) in June 1974, Taymor performed with Blau's group in Chicago and New York. The group disbanded at the end of the summer. And Julie Taymor, now twenty-one years old, set off on her next journey.

Indonesia

Taymor wanted to study visually oriented theater as well as experimental and traditional puppetry. With a Watson Fellowship to spend a year in Eastern Europe, Indonesia, and Japan, she arranged to stay on the Japanese island of Awaji, where a pre-Bunraku style of puppetry had survived, and where the masters would accept a female apprentice.

En route to Japan, she stopped in Amsterdam, where she saw the work of Henk Boerwinkel, one of the few artists then creating serious puppet theater for adults. She was particularly struck by his one-minute-long "haikulike" *Play*— which flipped instantly from comic to horrific and used audience reaction as its sound score. Taymor continued on to Prague and Italy, then headed for Indonesia, intending to spend three months there before moving on to Japan.

When she arrived in Jakarta, Taymor went to the national arts academy, Taman Ismail Marzuki. TIM gathered master artists from Indonesia's varied traditions of theater, dance, music, and puppetry. Here were the finest performers of the puppetry and masked dance that Taymor had sampled in Seattle, artists who could create a universe from shadows or could change their entire being as they put on a succession of carved wooden masks. The work ranged from the subtlest quivers of no-color silhouettes on a screen to extravaganzas of vibrant brocades and live blossoms. And it covered the spectrum from the utterly refined (*halus*) to the perfectly vulgar (*kasar*). Taymor was deeply affected by what she saw.

She went to Yogyakarta in Central Java to meet W. S. Rendra, one of Indonesia's most respected, and controversial, playwrights, directors, and novelists. Once there, she began to work with his Bengkel ("Repair Shop") Theater. A workshop for youths in trouble as well as an art collective, Rendra's group lived communally and created theater together. Lacking language (though she was functional in Indonesian after a few months), Taymor contributed to the work mainly as a choreographer, drawing on her LeCoq training.

What impressed Taymor most about Rendra's group was its relationship with the community. It rehearsed outdoors in a flat dirt area surrounded by banana and palm trees, with no walls. Neighbors, including children, stood or squatted at the edges to watch. This was startling, because the Blau workshop had been "so private, so interior, so precious, and nobody could watch until we were ready." Rendra's group played in stadia with audiences of two thousand men, women, and children, or in local village *sala* (open-air, public pavilions). This also was in refreshing contrast to the rarefied audiences of the Western avant-garde.

Rendra urged Taymor to create her own work. It was he, Taymor says, who recognized that she was fundamentally a director. And it was Indonesia that nurtured this dimension of her creativity.

Rendra supplied Taymor with actors, and before long a group of Indonesians began working at her house. At that point, she was living with an actor in a small compound with a dirt floor and a well, with no electricity or phone. She felt completely immersed in Indonesia and extraordinarily free.

For her first project, she explored two main themes: cultural transition and madness. The subject of cultural change was an obvious one. Not only was it the core of her present life, adjusting to Indonesia, but she saw it profoundly in the Indonesians' struggle between traditional village society and modern influences. And her preoccupation with insanity came from direct experience of how inadequately her own society had dealt with the "madness" of people she loved. In America, people on the brink were hidden away in institutions, but in some traditional cultures, including Indonesia, their energy was utilized as a creative force to mediate with the gods.

Taymor's trilogy, *Way of Snow*, started in frozen fields near the North Pole. Through the ritual of shamanic possession, an Eskimo was transported to the realm of Sedna, spirit goddess of sea beasts. In the second section, an Indonesian peasant's ox was killed by a bus, leaving the farmer screaming a silent, unhinged wail. Finally, in a modern metropolis, an answering-service operator plugging and unplugging wires went berserk. A psychiatrist removed disturbing items from her brain—including totems of the Eskimo shaman. In the end, the phone operator comforted and was comforted by an even more insane woman on the subway, a bag lady whose shadow was an image of Sedna.

The staging of *Way of Snow* showed theatrical tastes and skills that would color Taymor's work for years: formal elegance, filmic manipulation of scale and viewing angle, and a braiding together of global stage forms. The set consisted of half a dozen different-sized screens made of muslin stretched on bamboo. Four long, low panels suggested first a snowscape, then, with tiny palms, bamboo canes, and tufts of rice plants protruding from their tops, a lush Indonesian landscape. Turned vertically for the final section, the same flats evoked a city skyline. Meanwhile, larger square panels served as backdrops for masked characters and as shadow-puppet screens.

Action segued from mode to mode, using technique to underscore theme and creating a cinematic breadth that endowed three little stories with epic scope. When the Indonesian farmer and ox, played by masked actors, disappeared behind a large square screen, the focus shifted to the broad landscape formed by the low panels, where the farmer and other country folk now appeared as Javanese *wayang golek*-technique rod puppets. Eventually, they continued their journey as small relief puppets silhouetted against the large square screen, encountering carved leather shadow-puppet peasants on foot or pedaling bicycles. Before long, motorbikes, cars, trucks, and airplanes began to whiz across the frame at crazy angles in garish shades of blue, red, and orange. As these hard-edged Plexiglas vehicles blasted through the world of carved leather images, the fluttering oil lamp of the village section also changed to a harsh, electric beam. Horn blares and shouts invaded and finally replaced prancing gamelan music. Suddenly, the focus zoomed from this overview to a close-up of the farmer and his ox—who appeared again as masked actors in front of the screen. A cardboard bus knocked down the ox.

Another feature of Taymor's mature work that appeared in *Way of Snow* was a deft, barbed sense of humor. Her lunatic psychiatrist was Monty Python-esque, extracting from his patient such bizarre finds as hand tools and fish skeletons. Such offbeat, often black humor in Taymor's work offers respite from the serious drama while setting it in higher relief.

Taymor tried to give *Way of Snow* a ritual connection not only with its community but also with the land. She carved the wooden rod-puppets for the Indonesia section from a cotton tree outside her house. And the feathers that wafted down to represent snow in the Eskimo section came from the chicken the company had sacrificed and eaten as part of a traditional ritual to bless their project.

Though the piece may have had the favor of the metaphysical powers, it caused some stir among secular authorities. After performances garnered praise in Yogyakarta and then Jakarta (at TIM), the company was invited to perform at the arts academy in Bali. There, police stopped the performance. The label "Hidup Baru" ("new life"), written across the bus that killed the ox, was the very phrase used for government modernization programs. So, obviously, Taymor and the actors must be dissidents, probably Communists. She was taken in for interrogation. After her release, Taymor was invited to live and create theater in Bali.

Taymor's experiences during the next two years in the spiritually charged atmosphere of Bali shaped all her subsequent work. More immediately, they formed the center of *Tirai*, her next theater piece.

Shortly after she mounted *Way of Snow* in Bali, Taymor learned of a rare initiation ceremony to take place in the isolated Balinese village of Trunyan, near a live volcano, on Lake Batur. The village is one of the few communities of Bali Aga, or "Original Balinese," who consider themselves to have originated from the water itself, rather than from other parts of Asia. One of their unique traditions is an initiation ceremony for young boys that takes place once every five years.

Taymor set out for Trunyan with a performer from the Balinese *Way of Snow*, a part French, part Lebanese actor who had settled in Bali, and whom

Three wayang golek *(wooden rod puppets) from Part II of* Way of Snow, *set in Indonesia. Taymor carved them from a cotton tree outside her house in Yogyakarta.*

Taymor remembers only as "Roland." En route, a young woman they met invited them to a mountaintop ceremony. As they climbed the steep path, people passed carrying babies on their backs and ceremonial offerings piled high on their heads. But at the top, instead of the flower-decorated temple she had expected to find, Taymor was greeted by the most astonishing sight she had ever seen. The trees were filled with pigs. Villagers had suspended dozens of roasted suckling pigs from tree branches. That stunning vision proved the entry to a dizzying, several-day-long physical and spiritual odyssey.

Taymor and Roland arrived at Lake Batur several days before the initiation rites began. One morning, they climbed the volcano, scrambling up the lava rock in rubber thongs, clinging to roots, knowing they would never make it down the same way. After resting at the edge of a dormant crater, Roland headed around the rim to the live volcano, which was spewing every fifteen or twenty minutes. Terrified, Taymor followed. "To my right was sheer rock face, slate that would break off, and down to my left was the giant hole, and the wind was howling and shoving me. I crawled on my hands and knees straddling the rim— and when I came to the live volcano, Roland had disappeared into the sulphur smoke. I looked inside and I saw all the lava—yellow and red and white. And the next moment, I slipped. A piece of volcanic rock tore a chunk out of my leg. And the hole in my leg was the spitting image of the crater." When Roland finally returned, they washed the wound with tea from their canteen, wrapped it in cloth they tore from Roland's sarong and somehow made their way down to a village. Ignoring warnings to return to the capital, Denpasar, for treatment lest her wound fester, Taymor insisted on staying for the ceremony, and they headed across the lake to Trunyan. As evening fell, she settled herself under a tree in a square lit only by the full moon. She was completely alone—with the sounds of several gamelan orchestras coming from different corners of the village.

Suddenly a stream of elderly men appeared in full *baris* war dance costume, with bright brocade streamers and panels plus flower-festooned headdresses of carved leather. With no lighting except the moon, no accompaniment except their own guttural hoots, and no audience except Taymor sitting unseen in the shadows, they performed half an hour of *baris*. Only after they had finished did villagers come into the square to hang a theater curtain and set up propane lamps. An audience gathered and several artists did an *arja* dance-opera. Taymor realized that the *baris* had been for a nonhuman audience, for ritual communion with the gods. This performance recharged Taymor's awe at the root sacrality of theater. She felt how deeply Balinese art connects with its community, a community that encompasses not only the human but the divine. At that moment, her own work—aimed, like most Western art, at individual creative expression—seemed paltry by contrast. And her role as an artist, lonely.

This experience also impressed Taymor with the spirituality in the *act* of creation. Balinese dancers performing for no human audience, like shadow-puppet makers painting and gilding *wayang* that would be seen only in silhouette, made her understand how designing and crafting could themselves be acts of devotion. The process of creation was as vital as the end product. Twenty years later, Taymor would insist that costumes to be seen only from afar look perfect close up, that sets be finished beyond what spectators could possibly see.

The climactic event of the Trunyan initiation ceremony occurred the next day in the inner temple courtyard. As Taymor recalls it, the young initiates were dressed as sacred *Berutuk* forest spirits, in banana-leaf costumes and grotesque masks more typical of Africa or New Guinea than Bali. In a kind of ritual game, other villagers tried to entice the initiates over so they could steal a leaf, which brought good luck. But it was a dangerous venture, because the *Berutuk* wielded leather whips. This sacred sport continued in the temple for several days—with all comers in danger of being lashed except fathers with children and women with offerings piled high, who could pass unmolested through the charged space. Then, on the final day, the initiates ran amok through the streets of the village swinging poles and whips, beating everyone in their way. They ran down to the edge of the lake, took off their clothes, and submerged themselves.

But gnawing at Taymor's awe at the ceremony was her distress at Roland's behavior. He had thrown himself into the ritual, bartering most of his clothes to the forest spirits and becoming the center of attention. What he had done, she felt, was disrespectful and dangerous. That phenomenon of immersing and losing oneself in another culture, but on terms that violate the culture, became an important theme of *Tirai*.

After returning to Denpasar and getting her leg dressed at the hospital, Taymor settled down to sort out her experience and plan a new piece, possibly a film. *Way of Snow* had made her known in Bali, and the head of Peti Tenget village offered her the use of a bungalow that was part of an empty hotel on the beach. Built by Coca-Cola on sacred, taboo cremation ground, the hotel had never opened because no Balinese would work there. Writing in isolation in this ghost hotel, Taymor had two important visitors. The first was an American who had gone native and was living farther down the beach. A Vietnam vet, he examined her infected wound and said it was on the verge of gangrene. So, insanely, she let him operate, cutting down to the bone with no anaesthesia, pumping the cavity with antibiotics—and probably saving her leg. Meanwhile, she had become friends with a prominent Indonesian poet, Sitor Situmorang, who had recently been released from prison. One night, he arrived at her bungalow and warned her to return home. If she left now, he said, she would come back soon. If not, she was not only in physical danger from her wound but at spiritual risk of losing her bearings.

So, despite her confidence that she was "not the type" to founder, after two years in Indonesia, Taymor returned to Boston. She stayed home just long enough to have a doctor approve her front-porch surgery and to get a Ford Foundation grant to return to Indonesia and form a theater company.

On her way, Taymor stopped in Japan. She met with the Awaji puppet troupe, and saw traditional Noh and Bunraku as well as avant-garde theater. She found Japanese performance extraordinary, but felt it was on a pedestal, separated from everyday life. It lacked the connection to community that had so attracted her in Indonesia. She stayed only a month, then headed back to Indonesia.

Once in Jakarta, she immediately contracted hepatitis and spent several weeks convalescing at the home of the U.S. ambassador. Her friend Hadi Poernomo, a Javanese filmmaker, visited frequently. Together they planned and assembled a theater company of Javanese, Balinese, Sundanese, and Western actors. Poernomo obtained additional Ford Foundation money to support their project.

They called the group Teatr Loh ("the source," Taymor was told, in literary Balinese—and "oh my God!" in everyday Indonesian). They settled in Peti Tenget, living communally in two bungalows. For a year they held intensive workshops, with the artists teaching one another their various skills and traditions. Taymor calls this period her "trial by fire" in the theater. Tensions within the group came from the intensity and isolation of people from very different societies living together in a way that was untraditional for everybody. Moreover, they were doing deeply personal work that strained some of their own cultural traditions, and they were speaking Indonesian, the country's lingua franca but no one's first tongue. And though as a foreigner Taymor was outside the normal age-hierarchy, it was strange for experienced, well-established performers to be taking direction from a person half their age. Besides, women were supposed to be *halus*, refined, not assertive. ("If I were *halus*," Taymor once responded to a criticism, "I'd never get anything done!") Several members left— one young farmer/dancer saying he feared the work would pull loose his roots, others giving different reasons. Nearly everyone, including Taymor, almost quit at one time or another.

Finally, Teatr Loh harnessed these strains in a theater piece they called *Tirai*, which means "curtain." For Taymor, the piece was about boundaries: land boundaries, cultural differences, taboo, personal limitations, the boiling point before an eruption of anger or desire, the border where life crosses into death.[2] In contrast to the multiple modes of *Way of Snow*, *Tirai* used only masked and unmasked actors, juxtaposing naturalistic and stylized acting and dance.

Though the performers developed scenes through workshop exploration, the story came from Taymor's experience in Trunyan. A family of *topeng* dancers on their way to an initiation ceremony meets two foreigners, a Dutch geologist and a young American ex-marine (based on both Roland and Taymor's amateur surgeon). At the ceremony, the American thrusts himself into the rites and is nearly killed. In the end, the son of the *topeng* family leaves his family to follow the geologist. He has experienced what the young farmer who quit Teatr Loh feared: He no longer belongs either in his own culture or in the West. He is stranded in the middle.

Teatr Loh prepared to tour the piece, and Poernomo arranged for performances all over Indonesia. The Balinese company members spent three days praying in nine temples for a felicitous trip. On April 25, 1978, they took the night bus heading for Surabaya. Minutes after the bus pulled off the ferry onto the island of Java, they were hit head-on by a truck. The truck driver was killed, and every member of Teatr Loh was hurt, some badly. Taymor's chin and mouth were split open and glass was embedded in her neck. Poernomo suffered a serious back injury. Another dancer's leg was broken.

Teatr Loh members in rehearsal for Tirai *in Bali.*

Julie Taymor and the German actor Fred Maire as Ans (the Dutch geologist) and Zac (the ex-marine) in the Indonesian production of Tirai. *Here they have been duped into playing the weavers who are caught in a* topeng *version of "The Emperor's New Clothes."*

Nevertheless, a Balinese divining ceremony determined that the company possessed good karma. Big projects encounter big obstacles—and they had survived. So the group decided to patch itself up and continue. After being treated in Surabaya, Taymor returned briefly to America, while Poernomo looked after the company. The dancer with the broken leg was replaced by the daughter of the company's oldest member, Pak Made Tempo. Chastising the troupe's Balinese actors for having prayed using only Balinese rituals last time, a priest devised an elaborate blessing ceremony incorporating elements not only for the company's Balinese Hindus but also for its Muslims, Jews, Christians, and atheists. He then gave them holy water, which they carried with them on tour (in a Coke bottle). They opened in June and played in Java, Sumatra, and Bali. Before each show, Tempo, as company elder, led a blessing ceremony.

The tour sparked controversy. Traditionalists and government authorities, each for their own reasons, mistrusted work by a foreigner using Indonesian performance forms and dancers. To soften resistance, the group soft-pedaled Taymor's role and spotlighted Poernomo, the company manager, as much as possible. Still, *Tirai* provoked a range of impassioned responses from the arts communities and the Indonesian national press. One Balinese performer recently recalled, smiling: "People were not ready to see Pak Tempo half-naked."[3] On the other hand, a national magazine wrote, "Not only the play, but the entire project of Teatr Loh is an important event. A leading traditional actor like Made Tempo has the opportunity to express himself in a nontraditional way: a valuable experience in widening his vocabulary as a traditional dancer."[4]

That August, Taymor and Poernomo headed for Toraja, on the island of Sulawesi, to film a royal death-ceremony. Completing her roster of tropical disasters, Taymor saw this event through the haze of malarial fever. Her memories are extraordinary, and macabre. People in Toraja don't bury their dead but rather place wooden effigies with the bodies and then leave them out to decompose. So, walking through the forest, Taymor and Poernomo came upon a cluster of skulls and figurines. At the main ceremony, after days of ritual dancing, two dozen bulls tethered to boulders were to be slaughtered with machetes. But one bull wouldn't drop. "Black magic," an elderly man explained to Taymor, as the assigned machetier slashed again and again. Finally, she says, the bull broke free and lumbered down the hill to a microphone attached to a generator-run amplifier. "He got on the microphone and he started to roar at us. And it was amplified all around, bouncing off rocks and houses. And then the bull walked back up the hill and stood for a long moment, spurting blood, in the midst of all these dead animals. And then he rushed down at us, charged us. People, our cameras, went in the mud. He crashed into a house, which collapsed around him, and died."

After a week of feverish, gruesome hallucinations, Taymor returned to America. Though she has not gone back to Indonesia, her four years there left a profound imprint. Even much later productions, such as her Shakespeares and operas, that show no superficial debt to Indonesian techniques are stamped with the fundamental theatricality and balance she imbibed there. Her ability to sculpt together the monstrous, the sublime, and the trivial, without flattening any of them, has made her *Titus Andronicus* closer in a way to Balinese trance ritual than to traditional Western classical productions.

Back in New York, Taymor reworked and directed *Way of Snow* at the Ark Theater in June 1980, using American actors. With time to rethink the show and the use of more than a car battery's worth of electricity, she made several changes. In the Indonesia section, the accident became stunningly simple: once the farmer and ox reappeared as masked actors, a pair of electric beams glared through the screen. A crashing dissonance created the fatal accident, after which two red taillights receded. For the metropolis section, now called "New York City," she created the urban skyline with cut-out IBM cards on an overhead projector. Already Taymor was adapting what she had learned in Indonesia to the materials and sensibilities of home ground. The show, by a young, unknown director, opened to praises like "superlative," "brilliant," "virtuoso skill, . . . an ability to transform the mundane into the exceptional," and "images . . . so strong, so economical that [it] achieves the resonance of myth with almost childlike simplicity."[5]

Meanwhile, Ellen Stewart of La MaMa Etc. obtained funds to remount *Tirai*, bringing several actors from Indonesia. Taymor assembled a new cast that also included Javanese and Balinese performers based in America, a Korean, a Malaysian, and two Americans. Priscilla Smith, Andrei Serban's leading actress, played the geologist and Bill Irwin, the young American. *Tirai* played at La MaMa, and Dance Theater Workshop presented a program of intercultural clowning by members of the company. Both shows received acclaim—including my own response, after three exposures to Taymor's work, that she was "not merely a collector of exotic traditions but a first-rate director."[6]

Design Work and Psychodrama

Taymor quickly established herself in the American theater world—but in a niche narrower than she wanted. She became known as a visual theater artist who made innovative use of masks and puppets. Almost immediately after returning from Bali in 1978, she had landed an assignment in Baltimore designing sets, costumes, masks, and puppets for the Center Stage Young People's Theater production of *The Odyssey*. The show was directed by Jackson Phippin and opened in September 1979. Though Taymor was determined that her work not be ghettoized into children's theater, she felt that in this case she could create a show that, like Indonesian theater, would be aimed at people of all ages. Her *Odyssey* used an assortment of puppet types and scales. While Odysseus's little skiff got tossed around in an ocean of parachute cloth, tiny hand-puppet sirens, attached to the cloth, could pop up or disappear. Penelope, eternally waiting and weaving, appeared as an oversized head with heavy-lidded eyes plus a pair of moving arms, a style of puppetry Taymor had adapted from Peter Schumann's Bread and Puppet Theater; later, to greet the returning Odysseus, the same Penelope face appeared on a masked actress.

In her next project, *The Haggadah*, with director Elizabeth Swados at the New York Shakespeare Festival/Public Theater, Taymor's design work crossed into the kind of conceptualizing that is, really, directing. *The Haggadah* came from the desire of Shakespeare Festival director Joseph Papp to create an annual Passover pageant that would be culturally inclusive, not only Jewish. To support that vision, Taymor's theatrical Seder was an ecumenical smorgasbord. The basic staging recalled medieval Christian Passion plays, which arrayed multiple locales between hell and heaven: in this case, the extremities were an inverted pyramid with a serpentine pop-up Pharaoh and an asymmetrical Mt. Sinai. A giant Seder tablecloth later billowed up Peking Opera-style to become the Red

Two of Taymor's sketches for The Haggadah. *Top: The Angel of Death, which was a fifteen-foot-long puppet constructed out of tree branches and carried high in the air. Above: Moses. In this design, his hair and beard resembled a mass of Hebrew letters.*

The rabbis' wives, foam latex puppets, discuss recipes for the Seder meal in The Haggadah.

Sea. Life-size puppet rabbis debated fine points of Passover scholarship while women gossiped and compared Seder recipes. For the plagues, Taymor created colored Plexiglas shadow puppets: on high screens filling the theater's architectural arches, revolting reptiles chomped on humans, locusts swarmed and splatted as if against windows, and rats skittered out of their own archways to infest others.

By accident during this work, Taymor rediscovered an ancient form of puppetry. She noticed that light reflecting off the colored plastic plague figures threw clear images. From this, she developed "light puppets," using flexible mirrored Plexiglas to create images that seem to bend into three dimensions —a modern version of primitive mirror-stone reflections.

The *Haggadah* project received a lot of press attention, which contributed to the mixed-blessing view of Taymor as a gifted theater designer specializing in masks and puppets. It also brought her into contact with the composer Elliot Goldenthal. (A mutual acquaintance sent him to see Taymor's work, extolling it as "just as grotesque" as Goldenthal's own.) Over the next several years, these two would become primary artistic collaborators and, eventually, personal partners.

After *The Haggadah*, Taymor accepted a dozen other design projects— including a multimedia show at the Smithsonian Institution, masks for *Rashomon* at Smith College, sets and puppets for off-off-Broadway's *Talking Band*, masks for an off-Broadway *Midsummer Night's Dream*, scenery for the American Place Theater, and sets for a Broadway show. Although she found her auxiliary role increasingly frustrating, these assignments honed her art.

Black Elk Lives, presented at New York's Entermedia Theater in 1981, gave Taymor her first opportunity to design for a proscenium stage. She created a circle of tepees, whose conical outlines also implied the surrounding mountain landscape. On shadow screens (made by back-lighting tent fronts and a drum face) silhouette pictographs of buffalos and humans portrayed a history of the Native Americans. And light puppets of mirrored Plexiglas played out spirit tales.

Meanwhile, she was learning the "rules" of scene design—and which ones she could flout. Although actors complained that the stage for her *Black Elk Lives* was too steeply raked, they managed to perform on it, and Taymor was glad she had not known she "couldn't" use such a sharply slanted floor. Several years later, in fact, she would create a film set for *Fool's Fire* that slanted at an insane rake yet was workable for the action that would occur on it.

The same season, Jackson Phippin invited Taymor back to Center Stage to design costumes for a mainstage production of Christopher Hampton's *Savages*, a play about the annihilation of Brazil's Amazonian Indians. She wound up instead creating most of the actors. Her idea was to represent the Indians with

Painting the Brazilian Indian relief puppets for Savages.

23

larger-than-life bas-relief puppets. These forms, with few or no moving parts, would function less like puppets than like fully realized sculptures—strong, iconographic images. Her cast of oversized characters with beautifully planed faces and bodies included a mother and nursing baby, young men squatting on the ground, and a hunter with bow and arrow. Taymor later used such iconic relief images in shows she directed, including *Juan Darién*. The mestizos in *Savages*, halfway between the Indian and White worlds, were masked actors. And Taymor again visualized a series of Indian legends via the mysterious, spiritlike medium of mirrored Plexiglas reflections.

Next came a Broadway offer—scenery for a musical of *The Little Prince*. She conceived a phantasmagoric cosmos. The stage floor, covered with stretch fabric and controlled by hydraulic lifts, changed into a variety of desert land-scapes as sections of it rose and fell. Planets flew through space with live actors inside and puppets on top. For the plane crash, a tiny airplane whizzed (along a wire) from the back of the audience and smashed through the covered pro-scenium, which then opened to reveal the wreck in close-up—that is, a giant forced-perspective version of the plane.

But, with the show's planning well under way, the producers fired the director. Taymor did not get on with the new team. The director insisted on having a full-scale plane on stage, even though he would be stuck with it there until the act curtain. The choreographer objected to Taymor's aerial ballet of planes atop long poles because "I don't like my dancers using props." Finally, amid such disputes, the producers fired Taymor. Such vindication as she may have felt at seeing the show close before opening night was poor compensation for having the set design she felt was her best go to waste. When the same producers asked her to direct *The Little Prince* a year later, she turned it down.

After *The Little Prince*, Taymor had had enough of designing for other people. In the spring of 1984, she directed her first version of *The Transposed Heads*. She then spent three weeks in July working on an original script in the Playwright's Lab of Sundance Institute in Park City, Utah. Just as her career was gaining steam in these new directions, she was asked to design the set, masks, and puppets for *The King Stag*, to be directed by Andrei Serban at American Repertory Theater in Cambridge that fall. The prospect of working with Serban interested her enough to take on one last design project. She recommended Elliot Goldenthal to Serban, who engaged him to compose music for the show.

Carlo Gozzi's ersatz-Oriental commedia dell'arte fantasy offered a perfect vehicle for Taymor's art. A wicked prime minister, having tricked King Deramo into leaving his own body, usurps power by inhabiting it. In Taymor's designs, Deramo's face was transformed on the imposter (by means of a new mask) into a bloated, misshapen version of the same features. The true king, meanwhile, is trapped in other bodies: first a stag, for which Taymor created a life-size deer out of silk on rattan frames; then a crippled old man, which she cast as a Bunraku-type puppet. Taymor filled out this world with dragonflies and butterflies dangling from poles, mirrored Plexiglas light puppets of forest creatures, and fancifully masked humans.

Since her masks implied entire physical characters, Taymor wound up also creating the costumes and choreography for *The King Stag*. Besides indicating character, her stylized costumes spiked the action with humor. The evil prime minister's black cape opened out like bat wings. A wannabe court lady, Smeraldina, sported a rattan hoop frame covered with hankie-sized swatches of color, but no actual skirt.

Puppets always tease an audience about the nature of identity and aliveness. Taymor raised that ante here, challenging viewers to daredevil suspensions of disbelief: The protagonist was first a masked actor, then was contained in a bit of cloth and rattan, and still later was played by a Bunraku doll. When the king's bride (a masked actress) cradled her husband, trapped in the body of a crippled old man (a Bunraku doll), the audience had to make leap of imagination not very different from the bride's.

In Serban's directing, Taymor saw a foil to her own approach. While she always came into her first rehearsal having mapped out an interpretation in detail, his work was more spontaneous, more shaped by inspirations in rehearsal. She was not inclined to adopt that approach—partly because she *liked* conceptualizing in advance, partly because she was less quick to throw out design elements she had conceived and in some cases built herself. Still, she admired Serban's willingness to take wild risks, to toss everything upside-down to follow out an idea. And she enjoyed the collaboration. But it was all the more clear to her after *The King Stag* that the design seat felt too confining.

During this period, Taymor participated in one other project totally different from all her work before and since, but which reaffirmed her awe at the power of the mask. Dr. Ferruccio DiCori, a psychiatrist experimenting with psychodrama, asked Taymor to create archetypal masks—the overbearing mother, the benevolent patriarch, the bully, the victim, and so forth—to use with patients. She also worked with him on and off for several months in a public psychiatric hospital, doing role-playing therapy with the patients. DiCori videotaped the sessions using a live monitor so that patients could see themselves as they were working.

One encounter stands out. A very handsome young man came into the room, full of attitude, and slunk down in a corner. After he described himself to DiCori as a happy-go-lucky, sexy, cool guy who was attractive to women, the doctor asked him to try on a mask that was the opposite of what he had described —a light green mask with a nerdish face, like a caterpillar's or a turtle's. Seeing his new countenance in the monitor, the man suddenly whimpered, "That's me"—and he began to transform. Taymor recalls: "His head sank into his chest, and his voice started to change—it became weak and shaky. He started to describe what a terrible human being he was." He begged them to remove the mask, and when DiCori took it off, Taymor says, "the man's face was identical to the mask—sunken, sad." Slowly, then, he started to jerk his face and body back, like a beach ball reinflating, into the persona that he presented to the world. Taymor later found out that the man had been brought to the hospital the previous night after being talked down from a ledge of the Brooklyn Bridge.

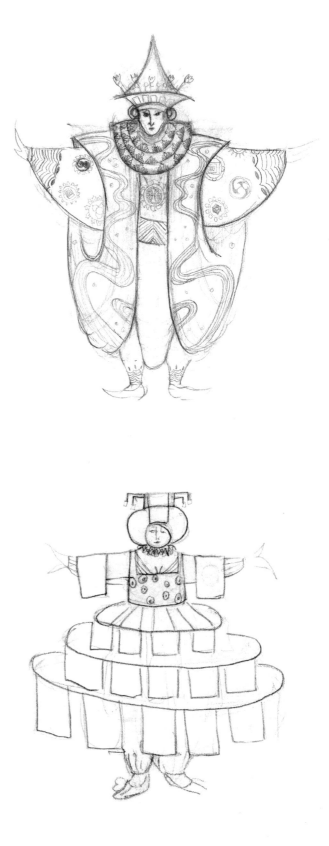

Taymor's sketches for King Deramo and Smeraldina, two characters in The King Stag.

Taymor's work with psychodrama connected with her concern about the nature of madness, of people on the brink. And it reaffirmed the astounding power of masks. "If you can put on another face, you can hide your own persona, and other parts that are locked away will be able gain expression—which is why masks are liberating for the actor."

Directing Original Adaptations

What Herbert Blau and, presumably, W. S. Rendra saw in Julie Taymor even before she fully realized it herself was that her fervor to generate physical stage forms was rooted in a creativity of *mind*. She was not just an inventor of impressive stage effects, but someone who used theater to express ideas and feelings. She was fundamentally a playwright, in the literal sense of "maker" of plays. After creating her own work in Indonesia for four years and then designing for other people, she began adapting nontheater pieces for the stage and directing them herself.

Her first project was a commission by the Ark Theater to adapt Thomas Mann's *The Transposed Heads* into a play to open in the spring of 1984. The German novella, drawn from an Indian legend, was appealingly cross-cultural, and its story—about two friends whose heads wind up by mistake on one another's bodies—invited the use of masks and puppets. Taymor wanted her *Transposed Heads* to employ movement and visuals as equal partners with language in conveying the story, as Indonesian theater often did. She and author Sidney Goldfarb wrote the script, based partly on actor improvisations, and Yukio Tsuji and Masa Imamura composed incidental music.

Taymor worked with the performers to find ideographs that would capture the story's essence. One gesture they developed showed the two friends, Shridaman and Nanda, holding on to each other's arms and leaning backward, each man providing support for the other. Later, when jealousy unsettled the friendship, the balance faltered. With designer Atsushi Moriyasu, Taymor selected visual techniques for *The Transposed Heads* to underscore its themes. The "scenery" consisted of mysterious, floating three-dimensional images—created by artist Caterina Bertolotto by projecting abstract shapes on a moving cloth maze. The effect, like a gigantic, evanescent hologram, presented the audience with a world that was exquisite but impossible to figure out—just right for a story in which reality cannot be pinned down. Face- and body-masks and puppets heightened the story's point about the ambiguity of identity. When the two friends, in love with one woman, Sita, decapitated themselves, Taymor showed their severed heads floating through space. But when the characters were incorrectly reassembled, it was clearly the *bodies* that were masks (the formerly scrawny Shridaman now sporting a set of prosthetic muscles and Nanda's erstwhile brawn hidden inside a "mask" of baggy clothes). Like the bewildered Sita, who can't decide whether the man with Shridaman's head or the man with Shridaman's body is her husband, the audience was left wonderfully perplexed about what was who.

Two years after the Ark production, Taymor undertook to redo *The Transposed Heads* as a musical for the American Music Theater Festival in Philadelphia. Elliot Goldenthal composed a new score of songs, recitative, and background music. The sounds swept from ethereal flute and hammer dulcimer tones to lyrical melodies to surges of percussive passion, reinforcing and sometimes layering humor onto the action.

This time Taymor worked with the scene designer Alexander Okun, former art director of the Moscow Art Theater. Okun placed the hologramlike maze inside a giant kaleidoscope—a fifteen-foot triangular tunnel of mirrored Plexiglas, which multiplied images into an infinity of illusion. Taymor liked not only the look of this set-piece but also its literalness. This was the first of many times she would take an element of theme or verbal imagery—here, the love triangle and the illusoriness of reality—and visualize it verbatim on stage, endowing it with iconic weight.

After opening in Philadelphia in September 1986, *The Transposed Heads* was cut down physically to fit into the small, thrust-stage Mitzi Newhouse Theater at New York's Lincoln Center for a two-week run. The reviews ranged from equivocal to ecstatic. Writing in *The Village Voice* about the first version, critic Alisa Solomon said, "The production compels complete submission to its magical effect. . . . It is contemplative and athletic, intelligent and sexy"; she particularly praised Taymor for heeding "the soul" as well as "the image" in Mann's story." *Washington Post* critic Joseph McLellan praised the musical version as "one of the most intensely theatrical experiences I have ever enjoyed."[7]

While she was fashioning cross-cultural and exotic stage worlds, Taymor also had been developing a project that was pure Americana. She had come across a reprint of the 1787 *Adventures of Jonathan Corncob, Loyal American Refugee*—an anonymous, irreverent tale (published in England) about an apolitical scamp at the time of the American Revolution. Its young hero fornicates his way through the war (getting seven kinds of VD) and, avoiding service in the colonial army, becomes a shipboard profiteer. Filled with battles, shipwrecks, and whorehouses, the story had the sort of epic scope that Taymor loved. And it was American—home territory, and an antidote to the pigeonholing of her work as Asian.

Taymor sent the book to David Suehsdorf, whom she had known since Oberlin, suggesting they coadapt it into a musical and he write the book and lyrics. On the recommendation of Ming Cho Lee, she contacted a recent Yale Drama School design graduate, G. W. Mercier, who became Taymor's collaborator on this project plus half a dozen others. And she asked Elliot Goldenthal to compose the music.

Taymor presented the basic idea of *Liberty's Taken* to Wynn Handman, head of the American Place Theater in New York, who promptly commissioned the piece. He also told Taymor about a biography of a colonial woman named Deborah Sampson Gannett, who had disguised herself as a man in order to join the Revolutionary army. This story completed the picture. Here were the two sides of the American character: the out-for-himself capitalist and the idealist.

Taymor, Elliot Goldenthal, and David Suehsdorf at work on their musical, Liberty's Taken.

The rocky romance between Jonathan and Susannah Wills (the character based on Gannett) became not only the spine of Taymor's plot but also her symbol of America's complicated spirit.

Taymor made *Liberty's Taken* a picaresque extravaganza—a kind of *Tom Jones* and *Birth of a Nation* rolled into one. Besides Corncob and Wills, she and Suehsdorf included a third main character, Desire Slawbank, Corncob's hometown squeeze, whom he leaves pregnant at the altar. While Wills fights for the rebel cause and Corncob seeks his fortune, Desire searches for her Johnny—only to be misused by every man she meets (except the disguised Wills, with whom she falls in love). The story moves from Virtue Falls, Massachusetts, to Boston, to New York, to the wilds of New Jersey, to the high seas, to Barbados. Its cast of a hundred and fifty includes pampered aristocrats, poor farmhands, and sad-eyed, abused slaves.

While unmasked actors played the three leads, fewer than twenty other performers handled all the rest using masks and puppets that commented on the characters. Corncob's wealthy, amoral old uncle, Mr. Winters, sported a self-satisfied, fleshy face, a powdered wig, and an outsized hand, each finger able to grasp and grab. The chief of the "Boston Committee of Safety," the morality police, had the stooped body and long-snouted silhouette of a rodent, and one large hand with a permanently pointing finger.

To achieve Cecil B. DeMille proportions, Taymor often had actors play multiple characters at once, and even scenery. Two thirds of the enlistees in Susannah's rag-tag unit were dummies: the miserable specimens played by masked actors had even more pitiful-looking stuffed soldiers attached on either

Mrs. Donewell

Taymor sculpting "The Havoc," a talking ship's figurehead, and heads for the Donewells, a family of Tories, in Liberty's Taken. *Her sketches for various characters in the musical are on this and the following page.*

Dr. Pompidou,
the saw-toting surgeon

An American sea captain

A British sea captain

The chief of the Boston Committee of Safety

side of them (making the fancy drills choreographed by Kimi Okada especially fun). The Boston Committee of Safety consisted of a host of painted plywood heads attached to a wheeled trolley, moving in idiotic unison, and surprisingly menacing. To create a field-hospital ward, Taymor had actors *wear* the patients' beds and puppet bodies.

Taymor and Mercier drew on American folk art for the visual imagery in *Liberty's Taken.* The play opened and closed with the stage's huge back wall depicting a patchwork quilt, sections of which flipped into doors, windows, and sky as the story unfolded. A Punch and Judy-style puppet show roved the streets of Boston. And Susannah's lecherous, tyrannical captain rode a wooden hobbyhorse.

Taymor exploited the virtuosity of puppets to add both physical and thematic dimension to several scenes. For a battle at sea, two small shadow-puppet ships in a back-lit panel of the rear wall heaved and pitched in the waves. Meanwhile, downstage, two giant figureheads bobbed on the ends of seesaws, which were manned at the opposite ends by the ships' captains. The effect was a screen-in-screen, wide-angle shot and close-up at once. Later, when starving troops shot and ate the hobbyhorse, the obvious fakeness and the humor disarmed the audience's defenses against taking in the horror of the action, but at the same time, the sight of men chewing on wood expressed awful desperation.

Taymor, Suehsdorf, Goldenthal, and Mercier filled *Liberty's Taken* with comedy, often dark. A sweet Tory lass adores stories of war gore. A saw-toting, lunatic surgeon can't get his fill of amputating—hacking off limbs even to cure fever. Humor was also built into the scenery. The hospital *beds* could dance a production number. A New York brothel, shaped like a gargantuan, voluptuous woman, had copulating shadow puppets in its belly and roll-out beds sliding out from between its legs.

Goldenthal's music helped modulate the play's shifting tone. Ranging from a cappella solos to elaborate orchestral scorings, it included lyrical ballads, Appalachianesque, Kurt Weill-like *spiels*, and zany fusses of dissonance.

The American Place Theater commissioned *Liberty's Taken* but could not, finally, afford to mount a production. Four years after Taymor began work on the musical, it had its only showing—less than two weeks of performances in the outdoor theater at the Castle Hill Festival in Ipswich, Massachusetts, in 1985, attended by enthusiastic audiences, local reviewers, and hordes of mosquitoes and greenhead flies. One critic called the show "the most creative theater this reviewer has ever had the pleasure of experiencing"; another deemed it "worth three hours and 1000 bites."[8] Taymor wants to mount the show again, in open run. But for now it remains a Taymor classic that practically no one saw.

A year after *Liberty's Taken*, Taymor and Goldenthal received a call from Lyn Austin, artistic director of the Music Theater Group in New York, asking them to propose a show. They described the story of "Juan Darién," and though they explained that nothing existed yet except their basic ideas to adapt the piece, Austin commissioned it on the phone and set an opening date. The result was a collaboration that packed all the talent Taymor and Goldenthal had been honing for years into a dense, spectacular—and dark—jewel of music theater.

"Juan Darién" was a Uruguayan short story by Horacio Quiroga that had haunted Goldenthal since he had read it years earlier while teaching himself Spanish. A disturbing tale of "savagery" versus "civilization," it shows a bereaved mother's compassion transforming an orphaned jaguar cub into a human child—and then her neighbors' fear and cruelty changing him back to a jungle beast. Goldenthal felt the story could be the heart of a Mass, and when he first saw Taymor's work on *The Haggadah*, he suggested they do *Juan* together.

Taymor directing Juan Darién.

Sketches for Juan Darién: *Mr. Bones and the schoolteacher.*

A week after their conversation with Austin, Taymor and Goldenthal traveled to Mexico. They spent several months in regions where Native American cultures were strong and Spanish was a second language, and they worked out an adaptation. They decided to express the story through music and visuals; the words, nearly all sung, would be Latin and Spanish. This would keep the life of the piece on a purely emotional plane, bypassing the intellectual. Taymor designed puppets and masks and called on G. W. Mercier to codesign sets and costumes with her.

Goldenthal wrote the music, carrying through his idea of *Juan* as a Requiem Mass. The score mixed refinement and rawness, weaving plainchant melodies and church harmonies through a composition for brass, keyboards, Japanese taiko drums, African shakers, Australian aborigine didgeridoos, and South American clay pipes and flutes.

Taymor created the chiseled intensity of the *Juan Darién* mise-en-scène partly by using techniques already in her repertory. Oversized bas-relief mourners that appeared around the stage while a tiny funeral procession threaded through her miniature village were the same sort of icons as the bas-relief Indians in *Savages*. To show a menacing hunter, she used a version of head-and-hand masks—in this case giving the hunter oversized, brawny, rifle-toting arms. Juan's terrifying nine-foot-tall schoolteacher was a grotesque kinsman to the chief of the Boston Committee of Safety, pointing a giant, bony finger and sprouting book pages for hair. As in *Way of Snow* and *Liberty's Taken*, Taymor manipulated audience perspective much as film directors would, inventing live-stage equivalents of changes in camera angle or lens focal length.

She also used methods not in her prior work. She fashioned a jungle with suspended valances of painted tropical flora. To create a sinister dancing skeleton, she crafted a weird cross between Javanese rod puppets and Japanese *kuruma ningyo* dolls, rigging the head, torso, and limbs of "Mr. Bones" to corresponding parts of the black-clad actor who stood behind him. When Leonard Petit, rehearsing Mr. Bones, improvised a romantic dance with an old-lady character, it was so chilling that Taymor incorporated the dance into the play, and Goldenthal wrote music for it. She was learning to be open to reshuffling her ideas to incorporate fortuitous surprises.

Since *Juan* is *about* what it means to be human, Taymor took advantage of the ability of puppets to tease at that border. The audience saw Juan change from a little Bunraku-technique jaguar, to a small wooden baby, to a Bunraku puppet boy—all interacting with the masked actress playing Juan's mother. When the mother died, she fell out of her mask, which was caught by an unmasked boy, and the character of Juan passed into this child, the first actual human face the audience had seen. From that point on, Juan, the transformed jaguar, remained the only character on stage with a real human face. The "human" society persecuting him appeared as a band of grotesques.

Juan Darién counterpointed the solemn with the comic, the tragic with the trashy. The schoolteacher and a macho carnival-barker were loony caricatures advancing the serious action. And Taymor crafted a series of scatological shadow-puppet farces—entertainments presented by Mr. Bones playing emcee at especially intense moments, for no logical plot reason. These "Tiger Tales" portrayed the eternal battle between humans and jaguars: a wild cat eats a cobbler, whose hammer and boots stomp in its belly and finally burst out its mouth and anus; a jaguar disguised as a man seduces a sexy dame, who turns out to be a transvestite packing a pistol for a penis. Taymor and Goldenthal wanted these interludes to undercut the story's sentimentality. The Tiger Tales also lowered the audience's emotional guard, so that *Juan's* brutal moments hit undefended targets. In fact, the dramatic equilibrium they created paralleled the Balinese notion of refined and crude, of *halus* and *kasar*, the elements that make up human life, without which no image of the world is honest or complete.

Juan Darién played first in March 1988, in the small performance space of St. Clement's Church in New York, and generated waves of excitement in the theater community. Mel Gussow wrote in *The New York Times*, "The play draws its power from the symbiosis of design, movement and music, melding diverse performance art forms and transforming the St. Clement's stage into a living theatrical organism. . . . In her previous theatrical work, Ms. Taymor has dealt with the theme of transformation but never with the artistic assurance and breathtaking intensity of 'Juan Darién.'"[9] Stephen Sondheim has described *Juan Darién* simply as "one of the best theater pieces I've ever seen." After the first New York run of *Juan Darién*, Harold Prince selected Taymor for the first Dorothy Chandler Performing Arts Award in theater, naming her the most promising stage artist for the next generation, and the MacArthur Foundation gave her one of its coveted "genius" grants.

After its initial run, *Juan Darién* was revived at St. Clement's in 1990, for two months of performances. It also toured to locations including Scotland, Japan, and Israel, sometimes playing in two-thousand-seat houses, and it garnered nearly a dozen awards, including two Obies. Now, Taymor and Sidney Goldfarb have completed the screenplay for *Juan's* next incarnation as a feature film.

Shakespeare

Meanwhile, Taymor had already begun to direct Shakespeare. She had not originally thought of herself as a director of the classics. While she resented being labeled by others, even she felt that her strength was creating concrete expressions in space, rather than interpreting language. Then, in 1986, she accepted Jeffrey Horowitz's invitation to direct *The Tempest* with Theatre for a New Audience, a company in New York that produces Shakespeare for non-traditional spectators. Taymor had designed *A Midsummer Night's Dream* for Horowitz two years earlier, and he thought that *The Tempest*, steeped in magic and illusion, would be a perfect match for her imaginative staging. Because the company often performed for schools, which imposed a time limit, Taymor and Horowitz abridged the play to ninety minutes. Goldenthal composed a score, and Taymor worked again with designer G. W. Mercier and Caterina Bertolotto, who had created the light-sculptures for *The Transposed Heads*.

Taymor and Elliot Goldenthal in a danse macabre with Mr. Bones.

Hal Prince presenting Taymor with the first Dorothy Chandler Performing Arts Award in theater, 1989.

For Taymor, the major new challenge was to find styles of acting that could support Shakespeare's extraordinary poetry yet remain moving on a simple human level. She devoted the early rehearsals to finding ideographs—essential, emblematic gestures. Her Prospero, Robert Stattel, looked for the movement that captured despair at the loss of one's library, one's source of knowledge, pleasure, and power. His ideograph—holding his hands together like a book, which then opened like a door, leaving him outside—used literal images to heighten the sense of his loss when those pictures dissolved. Ferdinand and Miranda searched for expressions of the discovery of physical desire. Ferdinand's gesture—running his right hand down his left arm, finally grasping the wrist—mixed sensuality, urgency, and wariness. Taymor and the actors used such iconographic forms to suggest the multiple layers within Shakespeare's drama: Miranda's words might express obedience to her father, while her movement revealed her longing for Ferdinand.

This poetic acting style also helped the human principals interact with the more eccentric characters, for whom Taymor used innovative masks. Ariel, a noncorporeal spirit, was a white, heart-shaped face with a shred of white silk for a body; an "invisible" actress (clad in black) spoke Ariel's lines and used her one white-gloved hand as Ariel's. For Caliban, an embodiment of brute force, Taymor took a literal cue from his complaint that "you sty me/In this hard rock" and imprisoned him in a stonelike mask, which he broke open when he believed himself freed. She gave the drunken clowns Trinculo and Stephano commedia dell'arte-style half-masks and exquisitely vulgar stage business.

The Tempest: *Caliban (Avery Brooks) cursing Prospero as he emerges from the black sand.*

To underscore the play's milieu of conjuring and illusion, virtually all the scenery after the opening shipwreck was crafted with light. Prospero's magic creations—the labyrinth, forest, and swamp in which he confounds the courtiers and clowns—appeared as insubstantial-looking landscapes floating in and out of existence, created by projections on moving layers of black scrim.

After its run at Theatre for a New Audience in the spring of 1986, *The Tempest* was revived for the Shakespeare Festival Theater in Stratford, Connecticut, in 1987, with a few cast changes and some text restored. Then Taymor reconstructed parts of the production for "Behind the Scenes," a PBS television show for young audiences. Taymor's first Shakespeare production received laudatory notices praising both its staging and its ideas. (My own mixed *Village Voice* review of the first version—in which I found it a bit breezy—was one of the few with reservations.) *New York Times* writer J. D. R. Bruckner called the first iteration "fresh, intelligent, and elegant"; Alvin Klein described the second, also in the *Times*, as "an intelligent, inventive production."[10]

As her next project for Theatre for a New Audience, Taymor chose *The Taming of the Shrew*, the Shakespeare she had performed in college. The main appeal of *Shrew* for her was that it concerned individuals interacting. It dealt with personalities and psychology. After so many shows involving created characters and metaphysical themes, Taymor wanted to do a play about regular people. Besides, she was anxious to direct a project with no fancy effects and no puppets or masks in order to break the stereotyping of her theater.

As she reexamined the play, she began to see a level deeper than the common view of it as a sexist tract. By giving Katherina the smartest dialogue in the play, Shakespeare had counterweighted the other characters' denigration of her and action that seemed to belittle her. Also, Sheila Dabney's robust, joyful audition rendering of Katherina's submission speech gave Taymor a new perspective: Kate so loved Petruchio for liberating her from her self-protective shell of nastiness that she could say those demeaning words publicly and not give a damn what people thought. With Dabney and the other actors, Taymor concentrated on pinpointing subtexts that often contradicted the characters' words, and finding ways to express those complexities.

Focusing on the psychological interactions, Taymor kept the mise-en-scène simple. (Also, the show was scheduled to move to a theater in the round, so there could be no high, solid scenery. Taymor did the original staging with the audience on two facing sides.) To support the play's earthiness, she wanted a Brueghel-Bosch feel to the designs. Catherine Zuber created period costumes. G. W. Mercier placed a high haystack stage-center for Shakespeare's pre-play (with the drunken tinker); then, for the play proper, the four sides of the haystack dropped, like storybook covers opening, leaving a roof supported by four thin posts. The inner surfaces of the sides now created four sloping floors, each painted in Sienese style with scenes of Verona—the city, fields, animals, and so forth.

The final two weeks of *Shrew* rehearsals, in March 1988, overlapped with the first two weeks of *Juan Darién* rehearsals. Then, making matters worse, the

Triplex Theater, where *Shrew* was playing, was gutted by fire during previews, and they had to move. Despite these difficulties, critics reviewing the show both in New York and the following month (with new leads) in Massachusetts spotlighted just what Taymor had aimed for: its straightforward presentation of psychologically complex characters. Clive Barnes, in *The New York Post*, called it "direct, sound, unfussy, and well-acted," pointing out that "the bluff Petruchio of Sam Tsoutsouvas . . . found a good match in the wary Katherina of Sheila Dabney." Stephen Holden's *New York Times* review described the protagonists as "intelligent combatants in a game of love in which both end up winners while the rest of the world watches mystified." Carolyn Clay, in *The Boston Phoenix*, described the Massachusetts production as "uncompromising, unsullied, and unsouped-up," crediting Taymor with having "dug beneath the play's woman-cracking-by-aversion-therapy surface to the root of the Kate-Petruchio alliance."[11]

It was six years before Taymor found the time and opportunity to direct another Shakespeare—again for Theatre for a New Audience. And although Taymor's *Titus Andronicus*, like so many of her shows, had only a short (sold-out) run, it was this production that established her as a major Shakespeare director.

Taymor saw *Titus* as an intricately constructed, profound statement about cruelty. And far from proffering the play, with its limb-lopping, progeny-cooking barbarism, as a period piece about Elizabethan or Roman appetites for gore, she cast it in a troublingly contemporary light. Presented in a year when TV news paraded images of atrocities in Bosnia and Rwanda, Taymor's *Titus* carried a clear and devastating message: Shakespeare's ultimate paradigm of inhumanity is our world. Moreover, we devour such brutality for entertainment. And this is the legacy we leave to future generations.

With set designer Derek McLane and costume designer Constance Hoffman, Taymor created a blend of styles that suggested a compendium of Western culture, from classical to punk. The main set-piece was a giant sheet of scratched plastic, with a black-and-white blowup of a Roman facade on a roll-

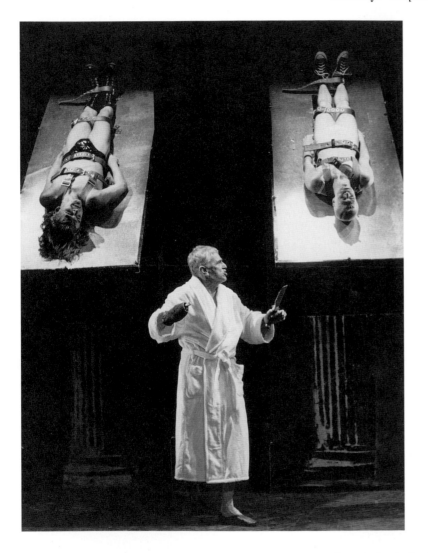

Titus (Robert Stattel) condemns his enemies, his daughter's rapists, to die. As he slits their throats, he pledges to bake them into pies to feed to their mother.

down shade in front of it. A footed bathtub served as a washing trough for Titus's Roman troops, a pit in the forest for Aaron's treachery, and a bathtub. Costumes, ranging from armor to hightops, constituted character and social commentaries: the ravished Lavinia spent most of the play in her torn, stained petticoat; white-haired Aemilius, a bureaucrat loyal to whoever holds power, looked like a U.S. senator in his tailored suit and tie.

Taymor layered on interpretive strata. She framed the action with the play's two children, Titus's grandson and the infant son of his enemies. Minor characters in Shakespeare's text, in Taymor's production the children are the point.

When the curtain rose, a boy in t-shirt and jeans played war at a Formica kitchen table. As sirens blared, he bashed soldiers together, doused them with ketchup, and then, increasingly frantic, hid under the table. That game done, he moved side-stage to watch (and play an extra in) the next battle entertainment: *Titus Andronicus*. Eventually, he entered the main action as Titus's grandson, young Lucius, then remained on stage through the final massacre, quietly watching—and learning. Meanwhile, Tamora's infant son, whom young Lucius's father had sworn to spare, appeared in the last scene in a tiny coffin. The final sounds as the lights went down were infants wailing, and then the screeching barks of birds of prey.

Equally unsettling was the show's suggestion that atrocity makes sensational diversion. Playing up *Titus* as an example as well as an exposé of savagery as entertainment, McLane gave St. Clement's black-box performance space a gold proscenium arch, closed by a red velvet curtain. Young Lucius's kitchen-table battlefield echoed the curtain's color and shape. As the carnage built, additional gold frames with red curtains appeared, presenting nightmare evocations of the main action: a dismembered body, the chest gasping its final breaths; Lavinia wearing a doe's head and being ravished by Tamora's sons, in tiger bodies. These frames stood out all the more because the sets and costumes were entirely black, blue, gray, and white, with very occasional blazes for red for Saturninus's smoking jacket and, of course, blood. The restricted palette inside the frames emphasized that the artifacts thus set off—including the play as a whole—were "artistic" creations being presented as entertainment. Indeed, on one occasion, a comic, blubbery henchman presented the attraction with the air of a sideshow barker. Meanwhile, Goldenthal's music—which generally fueled the show's jig between the edge of the unbearable and a curdled carnival—heightened the nightmare with crazed snatches of circus fanfare.

Rather than prevent the over-the-top gore from crossing (as it is wont) into farce, Taymor acknowledged the potential humor—not only to sharpen the barb that cruelty is entertaining but also to deepen characterizations. Having Robert Stattel endow some of Titus's madder ravings with a self-mocking wit gave him the dignity and complexity of self-awareness. The humor also fractured the audience's defenses, setting them up to feel the inhumanity that followed.

For all her attention to staging, Taymor saw the center of her task as directing performers. She spent nearly four months auditioning, and assembled a cast she loved. Then, according to Robert Stattel, Taymor guided the actors with a skill and sensitivity that had matured and deepened considerably in the years since their work together on *The Tempest*. Taymor devoted early rehearsals to searching for ideographic gestures that would convey both the scale of *Titus* and its humanity. She and the actors worked in particular with visual motifs from classic images of violence. Lavinia's futile attempt to avert her rape—entwined with her ravishers, arms reaching out, as she is dragged off—came from graceful Roman sculpture of the Rape of the Sabine Women. The Roman salute—hitting the chest and then raising the hand—became an especially potent emblem of power in this play where hands are so liberally amputated.

Though the Theatre for a New Audience's 1994 staging of *Titus* stands for the moment as another Taymor classic that practically nobody saw, the production's unusual, terrible power made an impact. While some reviewers were put off by the show's darkness, most waxed ecstatic (and, interestingly, several mentioned Fellini). Vincent Canby wrote in *The New York Times* that the production's effect was "hypnotic and sometimes genuinely scary." Julius Novick's *New York Newsday* piece captured the point succinctly: "Taymor succeeds in showing us that the world of 'Titus Andronicus,' where horror trembles on the brink of absurdity, has deep connections to the world in which, unless the daily newspapers are lying to us, we live."[12] Filmed excerpts of the show were incorporated into the PBS television series "In The Mix" as a catalyst for discussions of violence in contemporary society. One of the strongest Shakespeare productions in New York in years, Taymor's *Titus* is likely to get a new life. Plans are in motion for Taymor to redirect *Titus Andronicus* as a feature film.

Opera

Even for Seiji Ozawa, known in Japan as a maverick, hiring Julie Taymor to direct *Oedipus Rex* was a surprising move. The production would be part of the first annual Saito Kinen Festival, which he created for Japanese musicians scattered worldwide to work together each summer. He had first approached Akira Kurosawa to direct *Oedipus*, which was to be both performed live and filmed. When that did not pan out, he selected Taymor—a non-Japanese, female director, who was virtually unknown in Japan, had never directed an opera, had made only one film (for television), and whose work he had never seen live. But he liked the pictures he had seen of her work and her familiarity with Japanese theater. And he especially liked her ideas for staging *Oedipus*.

A rehearsal of Oedipus Rex *in Japan. From left to right: George Tsypin, the set designer; Peter Gelb, the producer; Taymor, the director; Seiji Ozawa, the conductor; and members of the Saito Kinen Orchestra.*

Jocasta (Jessye Norman) tries to prevent Oedipus (Philip Langridge) from realizing the truth of his parentage.

In fact, directing an opera was not a huge leap for Taymor. Nearly all her work had integrated music with drama. *Juan Darién* differed from "grand" opera only in scale. Still, directing a company of one hundred six (six principals, twenty dancers, and eighty chorus members) was different from handling a company of fifteen. And working with a fixed score and libretto and a cast she had not chosen would be new experiences. Also, opera aficionados warned her to expect trouble from the performers. Opera stars could be prima donnas and might well come in with inflexible ideas about how *Oedipus* should be done. In fact, Taymor was required to get her staging plan approved in advance by Jessye Norman, who was singing the role of Jocasta.

The Stravinsky/Cocteau *Oedipus* is an oratorio. It calls for masked performers standing still and singing out to the audience, so that no human trappings distract from the music and diminish its mythic quality. Taymor followed none of those directions. Instead, she turned the singers into larger-than-life figures equal to the fierce grandeur of the music. She placed "masks" atop the performers' heads like crowns, making the singers eight feet tall and leaving their faces visible. She also gave each principal character oversized hands and helped them develop ideographic gestures. Oedipus's raised hands, with outstretched fingers, would express benediction and, later, horror. Jocasta's gently curved hands would bespeak nurture and, later, dread. Creon's, with thumb and forefinger extended, would point accusingly.

Taymor added another dimension to the protagonist by double-casting a singing Oedipus, Philip Langridge, and a silent one, the Japanese experimental dancer Min Tanaka. Tanaka's startling, concentrated movement sometimes enacted Oedipus's past, sometimes portrayed what he described, sometimes

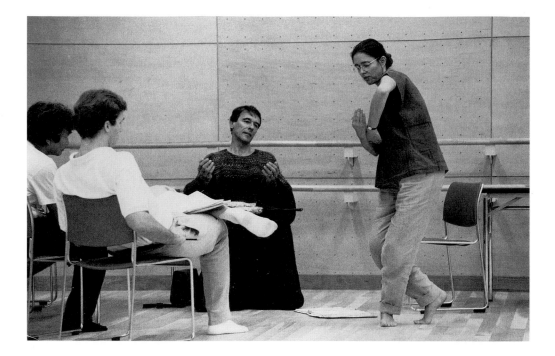

Seiji Ozawa, assistant conductor Dan Saunders, and Philip Langridge watch Taymor demonstrate a choreographed movement.

replicated his gestures, and sometimes counterpointed the text, revealing his inner torments or desires. At the climax, the two Oedipi fused, as Tanaka stabbed the eyes in Langridge's mask, then turned to reveal red cloth streaming from his own eyes.

To design the set Taymor chose George Tsypin, because she admired the boldness of his work. She wanted a stage world for *Oedipus* built of natural elements, especially water, which is so important in Japanese iconography and could underscore the drama's themes of pollution and purification. Tsypin designed a hillscape of wooden slats over a shallow, dark pool of water. He covered the huge back wall with gold-smeared metal screening bent into horizontal waves and folds, which could catch light in dramatic patterns.

Besides the moving actors, dancers, and chorus, only a few simple elements punctuated this magnificent starkness. Red cloth suspended Oedipus/Tanaka

Taymor works with Bryn Terfel to develop Creon's ideographs.

by the navel at the beginning, and later represented the three crossing roads where Oedipus slew his father. Clay-encrusted dancers lay clenched in rigor mortis in the water beneath the slats, while dark (puppet) vultures circled overhead. And most unsettling in its indistinct horror, Taymor's *Oedipus* began with the narrator slitting a huge rice-paper screen that covered the proscenium opening, giving the play's beginning a strange air of sexual violation.

Oedipus Rex calls for a narrator to introduce each section in the local language of the performance, summarizing the plot. Taymor's staging bridged the worlds of the Japanese narration and the Latin libretto and Greek story through visual images. The crown-masks, based on pre-Greek Cycladic sculpture, also looked like Japanese Haniwa tomb ceramics. The costumes, designed by Emi Wada (who had created costumes for Kurosawa's *Ran*) suggested both Greek cloaks and the geometric kimonos of Noh theater. Pale clay caking the faces and bodies of the chorus singers and dancers (to suggest the ravages of the plague) recalled the stone of the Cycladic sculpture and rocky cliffs—but also the white body paint of Japanese avant-garde Butoh performance.

Taymor's fears about prima donna stars proved groundless. When Norman saw the staging plan, she immediately understood the concept and said she loved it. The two women developed a mutual admiration during the course of a collaboration that Norman has called "exhilarating." She later described Taymor as "a true original, a great communicator, and an inspiration by example." Langridge, who learned about the unconventional production only when rehearsals began, also jumped in with enthusiasm. He was, in Taymor's words, "a consummate performer," working with her to develop his character's ideographs. Bryn Terfel, totally game, found the gestures for Creon very quickly— then carried on creating other ideographs, including John Wayne six-shooter moves, that kept the company cracking up during rehearsal breaks.

The chorus was another story. They neither knew Taymor's work nor in some cases were prepared to take direction from a woman (either Taymor or the Japanese choreographer Suzushi Hanayagi). She did not get full cooperation from some members until final rehearsals, when they saw the magnitude of the physical production and the stars' verve, and Ozawa was present to back her up. In the end, the dancers and chorus played a vital role in creating the torrential gravity of the production.

The opera opened in the presence of Japan's royal family, who allegedly had concocted a schedule of charitable visits in the area to justify the unorthodox trip. It was enthusiastically received and won the International Classical Music Award for Opera Production of the Year. Ozawa has described it as "one of the great experiences of my life, both from a musical and a theatrical perspective."

When she directed *Oedipus*, Taymor was already scheduled to direct *The Magic Flute* in Florence a year later. Zubin Mehta had seen a film and slide compendium of Taymor's work at the Dorothy Chandler Awards ceremony and then gone to a performance of *Juan Darién*. Based on those, he had asked her to direct his *Magic Flute* production, at the Maggio Musicale in Florence in summer 1993.

In Taymor's Magic Flute, *the priests of Sarastro play a Masonic chess game with the destinies of Tamino (Deon van der Walt) and Pamina (Mariella Devia), who are represented by small statues.*

Taymor worked again with George Tsypin and Caterina Bertolotto as well as with projections designer Wendall Harrington.

More than *Oedipus Rex*, *The Magic Flute* is a fixture of the opera repertory. It comes with two centuries of production history and accepted interpretation, including an overlay of charm, even cuteness. Taking her cues directly from the music and libretto, Taymor wanted to keep a fairy-tale quality but also to emphasize the opera's mysticism and darkness. After researching graphic symbolism in alchemy and Freemasonry, she proposed using a triangular kaleidoscope like the one in *The Transposed Heads* to underscore the libretto's mystical trios. Tsypin suggested they instead use four giant kaleidoscopes in basic geometric shapes: a triangle, a square, and two circles. They filled screens in the front and back of the kaleidoscopes and in the surrounding space with projections of magical signs from the zodiac, Tantric art, and other esoteric traditions. And they anchored the plot action in its various locales by projecting images of landscapes and castles.

Taymor felt that *The Magic Flute*, like *The King Stag*, defined an idiosyncratic, semimagic world, in which setting, characters' appearance, and movement must be of a piece. So besides directing, she designed costumes and puppets. (Her puppet codesigner, Michael Curry, handled the technical realizations of her conceptions.) To inhabit the strange universe of *The Magic Flute*, she drew more directly than before on the pool of her own creations. New versions of the silk stags and bear in *The King Stag* romped (with other beasts) in the forest. Her pig-footed Monostatos sported a bat cape like that of the evil prime minister in *The King Stag*. For the Queen of the Night's first appearance, Caterina Bertolotto created slides with thousands of tiny dots—a technique she had also used briefly in *The Tempest*—which turned the queen into a titanic iridescent moth. The queen's three ladies, wearing black except for one white-gloved hand and removable white masks *atop* their heads (which were concealed by black mesh), could function like Taymor's Ariel—as befitted their supernatural powers.

For Papageno's bird-catcher outfit, she designed a rattan frame, and she gave Papagena an uncovered hoop-frame rather like that of the silly court lady Smeraldina in *The King Stag*. Taymor hoped the audience would grasp in a nonliteral way that these two people were caged, confined by earthly needs for food, sex, and children. When they finally got together, they "undressed" one another down to their underwear—and wound up penned together in a larger coop that they shared with a brood of birds.

But the Papageno singer objected. Not grasping that the symbolic message was for the *audience*, not the character, he insisted that Papageno wasn't in a cage. In a way, Taymor sympathized with his uneasiness. After all, opera singers have often enough been made to look idiotic by directors with bright ideas. Still, she was frustrated. In her past work, when performers were uncomfortable with their costumes, the director had been able to entreat them "for the designer's sake" to try to work with the outfits. But this time Taymor was director and designer. So when Papageno began breaking pieces of the outfit during rehearsals, she modified it.

But that problem was the least of it. Some Italian chorus members were less than diligent about learning the German libretto. The stagehands worked six-hour shifts, so just when one group got things right a new crew had to re-learn everything. In principle, Tsypin's abstract set solved the practical challenge of the opera's two dozen scene changes, though the theater had to hire a bridge-building company to construct it. But the stage machinery in Florence's lovely old Teatro della Pergola was equipped to move painted wings and backdrops, not large, heavy pieces. Since Mozart had provided no music to cover set changes (the flat-scenery shifts of his time were very quick), Taymor was left gritting her teeth through long, noisy intervals.

Despite such frustrations, the production opened to enthusiastic reviews. Music critic Andrew Porter wrote, "We entered a world of beautiful surprises—entertaining, solemn, startling. This was stagecraft at its highest: technically resourceful, excellently rehearsed, exuberantly inventive, and never obliterating of Mozart's Music." The London *Financial Times* described it as "a fanciful, but never arbitrary staging that beguiled the eye and won the heart and, at the same time, set the spectator's mind to working." And *L'Opera* magazine deemed it "a personal triumph for Taymor."[13] And though its initial engagement in Florence included fewer than a dozen performances, operas, unlike theater productions, often have ongoing life. The production has been revived in Turin and is scheduled to play again in Florence. Taymor is also reconceiving the opera—including a new libretto—to be made into a feature film.

Even as she accepts other opera commissions—including *Salome* for the Kirov Opera, conducted by Valery Gergiev, and *The Flying Dutchman* for the Los Angeles Music Center in 1995—the piece Taymor is most anxious to stage is one she and Goldenthal have been developing since 1988. After *Juan Darién*, they wanted to create a full-scale opera. As a switch from the tropical climate of *Juan*, they selected a story set in the frozen north. Both had long been fascinated

Set designer George Tsypin with his model for The Flying Dutchman.

by John Gardner's *Grendel*, a retelling of Beowolf from the viewpoint of the monster. In contrast to Wagner's heroic dragon-slayers, their music-drama's protagonist would be the monster—the dispossessed, the outcast, the creature who observes humanity from the rim.

Part of the story's appeal was its sheer size, its epic scope. Taymor had liked *Juan Darién* best when it swelled to fill big theaters. And Goldenthal loves writing music for full orchestra—a desire he fulfills composing for feature films (his scores include *Drugstore Cowboy*, *Aliens III*, Oscar-nominated *Interview with the Vampire*, and *Ty Cobb*) but which the live stage can almost never accommodate. Their conception for *Grendel* is immense, thematically, scenically, and musically. They are cowriting the libretto, Goldenthal is composing the score, and Taymor devising the mise-en-scène for their monster opera.

Scenically, *Grendel* is by far Taymor's most elaborate conception. The winter landscape includes a floor of ice, on which beasts zoom at breakneck speed playing hockey with skulls and dead animals. The puppets range from shadow and mirrored Plexiglas light forms to a giant dragon that takes over the entire set. For the first time, Taymor uses film on stage—much of it animation. The opera begins with a forced-perspective, white winter mountain-scape, under which the monster hibernates. Gradually, through projection of hand-painted animation, spring arrives. Ice cracks, a river breaks through, and sap begins to run up trees, which sprout leaves, flowers, and fruit. Then *real* water starts to flow, and real fruit appears. Finally, a rock falls (loosened by a ram humping a stump) and lands on Grendel's head, awakening him. Taymor calls for a two-projector technique, to avoid the washout that comes from stage lighting in the microseconds between frames of a single-projector film. And, as she collects coproducers for this titanic project, aiming toward production in 1997 or 1998, she is conceiving it both as a live production and a movie.

Film

Since her Oberlin days, Taymor has been fascinated by the creative possibilities and challenges of the screen—including animation, shadow puppetry (which she sees as "primitive animation"), and movies. The appeal of the medium goes beyond aesthetics. Film and TV are the only American media whose audiences have the inclusiveness, the demographic variety, of Indonesian theater audiences. Also, unpersuaded by the romantic notion that the products of inspiration and sweat should exist for a few brief performances and then disappear, she finds the enduringness of film very appealing.

Taymor studied film at Oberlin and experimented with film and video in Bali and Japan. When she got back to America in 1979, she enrolled in film classes at New York University. Over the next few years, she became involved in film, video, and television projects with roles that varied from designing puppets to running cameras to writing scripts to directing. The ventures ran the gamut from documentaries about Asian performers to comic short subjects to television pilots to an MTV spot. And she spent a month at Sundance Institute's filmmaking lab in June 1990 as a "directing fellow" working on scenes from her screenplay for Poe short stories as well as a film treatment of *The Transposed Heads*.

Much as Taymor's stage work gains impact from techniques usually associated with film, her movie treatments often feature kinds of artifice more normally used in live theater. Sliding between real-looking and frankly sculptural or painterly worlds, she roots the fantastical in the everyday and reclothes the familiar in new layers of meaning.

Taymor's first major film project was an adaptation of Edgar Allan Poe's "Hop-Frog," aired on the PBS series "American Playhouse" in March 1992. In Poe's story, a dwarf called Hop-Frog, kidnapped from his family, is forced to amuse a "corpulent, oily" king and royal ministers. When a lovely midget, Trippetta, is brought to the palace as a new toy, Hop-Frog is moved to love, and then to a horrible revenge against their tormentors. Taymor had planned to pair "Hop-Frog," directed surrealistically with a menagerie of grotesques, and "The Tell-Tale Heart," cast with humans and filmed in black and white. The double-bill would show two sides of Poe and of her own work—contrasting a spectacular, external piece with a dark, psychological one. When budget constraints required dropping one of the stories, she kept "Hop-Frog"—or *Fool's Fire*, as they named the film version—because it could make a full-hour show.

Taymor induced the audience to identify with Poe's dwarf heroes by making them the sole humans in a cast of puppet caricatures. This also solved the dilemma that casting obese, ugly people as the royal entourage would be uncomfortably close to gawking at "freaks," as Poe's courtiers do. The only other real (or real-looking) creatures in *Fool's Fire* were stable animals and the fish and pheasant into which the puppet king and ministers sunk their knives and forks. Compounding this ironic play, Taymor gave the latex courtiers crude wooden dolls as sex-toys—then made these puppets' puppets the only beings to

Fool's Fire: *Taymor, in her loft, sculpts one of the minister figures, and Michael Curry, the character technical designer for the film, fits the king's bodysuit and mask on the actor.*

OPPOSITE: *Taymor's costume and face designs for Hop-Frog, the king, ministers, and a lady of the court, in Fool's Fire.*

shed tears for the abused Trippetta. Ultimately, this nontraditional casting helped make audiences feel the story's gross inhumanity and hideous violence even in a medium, television, where inhumanity and violence are routine: puppets somehow could navigate around the callouses of violence-hardened viewers.

To create an environment suited to both human and fabricated characters, Taymor and Mercier combined realistic scenic elements with sets that were obviously sculpted or were painted in the style of Giotto frescoes. For one set, the king's banquet hall, they translated Sienese painted perspective into three dimensions by crafting the room at a lunatic (forty-five-degree) rake, with the actors brought up into their positions through the floor.

G. W. Mercier with his model for the banquet scene of Fool's Fire.

Taymor exploited the camera's ability to control the spectator's point of view, both to facilitate scenic illusions and to mold the audience's sympathy. For scenes requiring enormous sets or huge casts, such as a grand ball, Taymor and Mercier designed miniatures that on film looked full scale. When Trippetta arrived at the court in a cage, Taymor had the camera slowly track completely around her cage in one long take, making the audience share Hop-Frog's mesmerization, its eyes locked onto the vision of Trippetta.

She used the wizardry of editing to create startling transitions. Often, she focused on a flat surface—a cabbage leaf, a painted castle exterior, a puppet-stage curtain—then opened it like a theater curtain, or storybook cover, to reveal the unexpected next scene behind it. And she shot a fifth of *Fool's Fire* in High Definition TV, which allows compositing images while shooting rather than in the editing room. This technology gave Taymor great freedom and control in piecing miniature and full-size elements into a single scene.

Taymor checking out a
shot during filming of the
royal bath sequence. Bobby
Bukowski, the director of
photography, is at the far left.

Actors and crew in between
shots on the set of the banquet scene in Fool's Fire.

The actors on a break during filming of Fool's Fire *connect to their "tubes of comfort" for some cool air. Left to right: Reg E. Cathey, Patrick O'Connell, Mireille Mossé, and Paul Kandel.*

For all the high-tech complexity in *Fool's Fire*, perhaps the worst problem during filming came from nature—in the form of one-hundred-plus degree August temperatures, made all the more stifling by the smell of live chickens and pigs in the studio for the stable scene. To provide some relief for the sweltering actors, the technical crew rigged air-conditioner hoses that could go inside the costume layers of latex and fabric. Still, the company had to break a few times to attend to performers who had passed out.

Another form of heat arrived in the fall after PBS officials saw the film. With the government arts funding under attack by conservatives in Congress, some public TV executives panicked—not at the extraordinary violence in *Fool's Fire* but at its bit of scatological language, specifically the king musing that "there's nothing like a well-downed goose to wipe your arse with." They insisted that the offending line, a quotation from Rabelais's *Gargantua*, be excised. Taymor objected. She wanted to emphasize the king's repulsiveness at every turn, to show what drove Hop-Frog over the edge. Also, the king's *kasar* behavior put the tenderness of the love story in keener perspective. In the end, PBS created an expurgated version "for use by stations who have their own community standards about what they consider airable."[14] Taymor's response was, "If they're going to start censoring on that level, they're going to have only the softest, most watered-down art on television. They're going to scare away anyone who has an edge."

Los Angeles Times critic Ray Loynd wrote, "What prepares you for this hour-long phantasmagoria are long-suppressed memories of childhood wonder . . . and, on the deepest level, emanations of terror and madness. . . . Taymor has dared to visualize Poe's dark, symbolist mind, leaving all prior Poe adapters in the dust."[15] Television producer Norman Lear, a longtime Taymor fan, has said that *Fool's Fire* opened new artistic ground for the medium. "She made a marvelous use of film to do something for the first time. She leads—there's nobody in front of her. And I'm trying hard to think who may be behind her. She needs a little more visibility to get that line started."

The next Taymor work to be shown on television, also on PBS, was that archetype of family violence and sexual abomination, *Oedipus Rex*—the film of the opera she had staged in Japan. In this case, Taymor did not reconceive the work. The two live performances in Japan were filmed and, in between, Taymor had five days to stage material specifically for the film, shooting behind the proscenium arch single-camera style with a steady-cam, dollies, and cranes.

Some elements of the live production would not translate well to the screen. In performance narrator Kayoko Shiraishi, standing still, could hold an audience with her intensity. But Taymor thought that such prolonged stasis in a movie would be tedious, so she blocked movement for Shiraishi (and the camera) through the set. A more intractable problem came from the mask-crowns. They made the principals' heads unusually high and narrow, while the film frame is wide and low. Forced, for close-up shots, to choose and move among a singer's real face, the mask, and a wider focus, Taymor turned the necessity to her advantage, zooming in with ferociously tight shots of a character's eyes and mouth.

With the camera able to shoot from within the set, Taymor filmed the principals and the chorus from various perspectives, in carefully orchestrated visual relationship with one another. The camera followed vultures circling down around individuals and led the audience slowly through the dank underbelly of Thebes, where corpses lay in misty pools, in Butoh postures of death agonies. Most spectacularly, Taymor staged a deluge at the end of the opera—with water falling the full height of the stage, through the slats, to the pools below. Because the water machinery clanked on noisily and the sound of falling water would have splashed into the music in live performance, Taymor could use this ending only in the film. There, after the final musical notes, Oedipus faces exile in a literal storm—and at the same time one feels that the weeping heavens are cleansing Thebes and restoring its life-giving forces.

When the film aired on PBS, *The New York Times* praised Taymor's work as adding "a significant dimension to Stravinsky's work, bringing resonance without distortion." It went on say that she had managed "to recapture the primitive energy once possessed by art."[16] *Oedipus Rex* garnered several awards, including an Emmy (for its costumes and body sculpture) and the Jury Prize at the Montreal Festival International du Film sur l'Art.

Taymor has also reconceived several of her theater projects that still feel fertile to her for the screen. She and Sidney Goldfarb have written a screenplay for *Juan Darién* that exploits the ability of film to slide between outer and interior realities, rooting their magical story in a real Latin American village. In this version, a traveling theater company performs the play of *Juan Darién*, while the real Juan, an orphaned street urchin, watches from the edge of the crowd. Then, partway through, like Alice going through the looking glass, Juan rushes into the story on stage. Taymor's idea for *The Transposed Heads* similarly uses film's

Taymor and Elliot Goldenthal at work on Grendel, *1994.*

facility to segue between naturalism and fantasy to create "normal" modern characters with whom an audience can identify but who wind up in a mysterious world where heads get lopped off and reattached. In this case, her screenplay bounces between Jackson Heights and Columbia University in New York, modern Bombay, and a surreal, fairy-tale India, which has scenery like Indian miniature painting and mysterious, supernatural characters.

Taymor's screenplay of *Titus* travels across continents and millennia. The two-thousand-year heritage of brutality that she suggested on stage with costume and set pieces appears more literally in the film, which leads the viewer through doors that connect The Bronx and the Roman Colosseum, Western culture's cradle of savagery as entertainment. *Titus* is likely to be Taymor's first feature film.

Harvesting existing art in order to cross-breed new work is one key to Taymor's creativity. Since her college studies of shamanism and "the primitive energy once possessed by art," Julie Taymor has searched backwards, forwards, sideways, through shadows, through reflections, among living creatures, among totems, in poetry, in philosophy, in music —everywhere—to find impulses for vital theatrical expression. Now, her own oeuvre has become part of the gene pool of inspiration on which she draws.

Developing in an artistic climate where Postmodern intellectualism made it fashionable to disconnect visceral from conceptual dimensions of art, her work has been exceptional not only in its excellence but in its aliveness. Certainly, her talent can integrate Indonesian, Italian, Japanese, and Greek elements in one picture. More important, it integrates language, thought, feeling, image, sound, and movement in an organic experience.

One secret of this vitality may be Taymor's artistic passion, her sheer pleasure in the process of making theater. Jessye Norman has remarked, "Julie loves what she undertakes, and the evidence is there to see and enjoy in every aspect of a production." And Elliot Goldenthal, her closest collaborator, when asked what drives Taymor, answered instantly, "I think it's the joy of creating. She really gets into a charismatic state—a heightened state—when she is creating something, and that joy is really, really there, and really true."

When Harold Prince presented Taymor with the first Dorothy Chandler Performing Arts Award in theater, he said, "When you spend thirty-five years in the theater you hope that you'll come across an unexpected talent that takes us in a new direction." What distinguishes Taymor's work is not just the new terrain she walks and the prodigious theatrical languages in her vocabulary. It's that she makes the space her own, and she transforms the languages—both to give new voice to old theater traditions and to sing her own song.

Notes

1. Harold Prince, speech presenting Taymor with the Dorothy Chandler Performing Arts Award in theater, Los Angeles Music Center, Dorothy Chandler Pavilion, September 12, 1989. From videotape of awards ceremony.

    Except as noted, all Taymor quotations come from personal communications with the author between 1987 and 1994, and all other quotations—including those by Herbert Blau, Elliot Goldenthal, Norman Lear, Jessye Norman, Seiji Ozawa, and Stephen Sondheim—come from personal communications with the author in 1994.
2. Julie Taymor, "Teatr Loh, Indonesia, 1977–8," *The Drama Review*, T82 (June 1979), p. 70.
3. Conversation with I Nyoman Catra, 1994.
4. *Tempo* (Indonesia), 1978. From Teatr Loh promotional material, 1979.
5. Tish Dace, "Way of Snow," *Other Stages*, June 12, 1980; Don Shewey, "Bali Highs," *SoHo News*, June 11, 1980, p. 12. Terry Curtis Fox, "No Strings," *The Village Voice*, June 25–July 1, 1980, pp. 77–78; Michiko Kakutani, "Stage: 'Way of Snow' Employs Masked Actors and Puppetry," *The New York Times*, June 21, 1980, p. 12.
6. Eileen Blumenthal, "Short Takes: Tirai," *The Village Voice*, November 26–December 2, 1980, p. 85.
7. Alisa Solomon, "Slings and Eros," *The Village Voice*, May 29, 1984, p. 89; Joseph McLellan, "Music: Duke Ellington's Operatic Encore," *Washington Post*, September 22, 1986, p. C-3.
8. Chris Young, "Taymor's Puppets Please All," *Lawrence Eagle Tribune*, July 11, 1985, and Arthur Friedman, "'Liberty' Worth Time and Bites," *The Boston Herald*, July 12, 1985.
9. Mel Gussow, "'Juan Darien' A Tragic Story Told Without Talk," *The New York Times*, March 16, 1988, p. C-24.
10. Eileen Blumenthal, "Squat Dreams," *The Village Voice*, March 18, 1986, p. 89; J. D. R. Bruckner, "Stage: 'The Tempest' at New Audience," *The New York Times*, March 27, 1986, p. C-15; Alvin Klein, "'The Tempest' Staged in Stratford," *The New York Times* (Connecticut edition), May 10, 1987.
11. Clive Barnes, "Barnstorming," *The New York Post*, March 14, 1988; Stephen Holden, "Stage: Taming of Shrew," *The New York Times*, February 16, 1988, p. C-19; Carolyn Clay, "Embraceable Shrew," *The Boston Phoenix*, April 29, 1988, Section 3, pp. 7, 15.
12. Vincent Canby, "Titus Andronicus", *The New York Times*, March 20, 1994, Section 2, p. 17; Julius Novick, "The Horrific World of 'Titus Andronicus,'" *New York Newsday*, March 21, 1994.
13. Andrew Porter, "On Platform Souls," *The Observer* (London), June 27, 1993; William Weaver, "The Magic Flute," *Financial Times* (London), June 22, 1993, p. 21; Davide Annachini, "Inexhaustibly Creative *Flute*," *L'Opera*, July–August 1993, p. 11.
14. Telephone conversation with Melinda Ward, Head of Cultural Programming, PBS, March 6, 1992.
15. Ray Loynd, "'Fool's Fire' a Fabulist Journey," *Los Angeles Times*, March 25, 1992, p. F-8.
16. Edward Rothstein, "Two Oedipuses, One Clad in Guilt, the Other in Clay," *The New York Times*, March 31, 1993, pp. C-15, C-20.

WAY OF SNOW

Written, directed, and designed by Julie Taymor

Produced in Java and Bali, 1974–75

New version produced at The Ark Theater, New York City, and International
Puppet Festival, Washington, D.C., 1980

Music by Gengi Ito and Dan Erkilla

Insanity, deprivation, shamanism, progress: themes of *Way of Snow*, my first
original work, had been taking shape in my mind for a number of years, but
not until my trip to Indonesia did all the parts come together.

Way of Snow tells of the struggle for both physical and spiritual survival
in three different worlds: Eskimo, Indonesia, and a metropolis. Conceived as a
mask-dance dramatic trilogy, it did not rely on language to propel its story.
As in silent film, imagery and music carried the action, thus enabling the piece
to cut across cultural boundary lines.

The first image we see is a white figure slowly twirling a plate on top of a
long pole, causing a snowstorm of white chicken feathers—the chicken, a sacrifice to another life. (In Indonesia, we had ritually sacrificed a chicken at the
beginning of our tour.) The way of snow, a paradox—each flake melts, yet snow,
falling incessantly, lays a bed that covers the tracks, buries the traces of memory.

Part I is set in the icy, barren landscape of the Eskimo. The chicken feathers
swirl to the ground, and fish skeletons protrude from the ice floes. The people
are starving and their shaman must make a spirit journey to Sedna, the goddess
of the sea beasts, to restore harmony between man and nature. Sedna's body,
a giant, intricately carved and painted leather shadow puppet, is a map whose
form evokes the legend of how her dog husband cut off her hand and threw it into
the sea, where her fingers became all different varieties of fish. The shaman's
ritual trance is successful and the people feast. A young boy falls ill, a sign that
he is chosen to become a shaman. During his "vision quest," guided by the elder
shaman, the initiate's spirit is overcome and his body dies in the wilderness.

In Part II, we are in the tropics of Indonesia. The icescape of the Eskimo,
the horizontal bamboo screens of stretched white muslin have sprouted the
green of palm trees and rice paddies. Nature is verdant, friendly, and productive.
Uncertainty sets in when a farmer heads to the city to sell his produce. Motor
vehicles of every conceivable type speed past his lumbering oxcart. The farmer
beats the ox to make it go faster. It cannot. He beats it again. Nature rebels.
Blood flows. Insects swarm and disease sets in. The ox sways into the road and
is hit by a speeding vehicle, which hurries on unconcerned. The farmer rages
after the disappearing taillights.

*The initiate, who takes a "vision quest"
in the Eskimo snowfields.*

55

Part III takes place in a metropolis. The frozen concrete forms of the sky-scrapers resemble the frozen wasteland of the north, except that the shapes are now vertical rather than low and horizontal. An answering-service operator succumbs to the isolation and monotony of her job. She goes out of her mind, losing control of her own self as, literally, her alter ego (a small puppet-double that she has been manipulating just as her headset has been manipulating her) rebels and leaps out the window. Her hallucination takes her on a journey to the moon, much like the shamans' in Part I, only she is unguided and crashes to the earth. Seeking help, she finds herself in the office of a modern-day shaman, a psychiatrist, who operates on her brain, extracting all unnecessary and inexplicable items—boats, fishbones, palm trees, and so on. He replaces them with a clock and a giant torpedo-shaped pill. The final image is of the woman on an endless ride in the subterranean/celestial subway where she meets Sedna, now in the form of a lunatic bag-lady. The young woman lays her head on Sedna's lap and, suddenly, out of the old woman's sack emerges the little figure of the operator, her spirit, which she thought she had lost forever.

Spiritual starvation replaces physical starvation as the piece moves from the northern snowfields to the city. Whereas the shaman sought to lead his "patient" *through* sickness and imbalance to a position of greater strength and wisdom, the psychiatrist attempts to rout out the deviant and destructive behavior and render the patient normal, adjusted. Her insanity is not tapped for its creative powers as in a tribal culture that has a forum for those with such "gifts." She, instead, is destroyed. Part II, in Indonesia, has no shaman/psychiatrist figure because it is about transition from an ancient, traditional world view to a modern one and the illness has yet to be recognized.

I selected techniques for *Way of Snow* for their inherent meaning as well as the poetry of their expressiveness. The materials used for Part I included wood, stone, and leather, and the illumination came primarily from fire. By Part III, I was using an overhead projection of IBM cards to represent the city skyline.

The transition from traditional materials to high-tech ones occurred in the shadow-play sequence in Part II, where the farmer travels from country to city. Intricately carved leather shadow-puppets of characters on foot, on bicycle, or in horse-drawn buggies, lit by a flickering oil lamp (fire, the symbol of life) were overcome by brightly colored Plexiglas shadow puppets of motorcycles, cars, trucks, and planes, lit by an electric bulb. The light assaulted with a hard-edged and dynamic tone as the scene shifted from village to city. Unlike the leather puppets, which had visible detailed moving parts, the Plexi puppets had no moving parts, as they moved too fast for the detail to be seen. In Indonesia, this aspect of the production was highly sensitive and controversial, as it high-lighted the dilemma in which unique qualities are lost as old traditions are replaced with new technologies.

Taymor as the white shaman who steals the spirit of the initiate in Part I, which takes place in the land of the Eskimo.

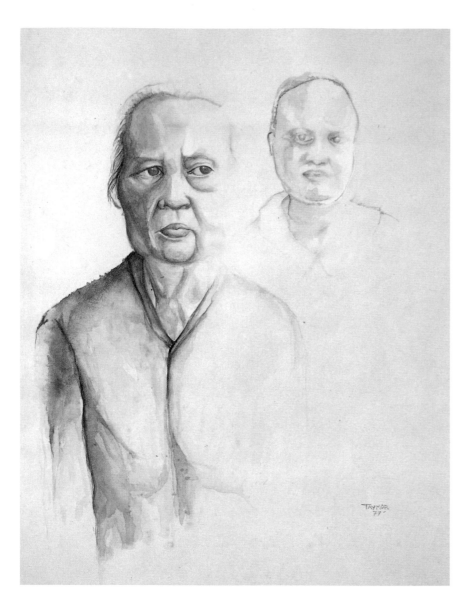

During her four years in Indonesia, Taymor sketched and painted everywhere she went—in trains, in markets, at temple performances. These faces became studies for the characters she would create for her plays.

OPPOSITE BOTTOM: *Leather shadow-puppets used for the road scene in the Indonesian section.*

LEFT: *In Part III of the trilogy, the New York City answering-service operator manipulates "herself."*

BELOW: *The actor Suharno manipulating Sedna, the Eskimo goddess of sea beasts. She is carved from buffalo hide and painted in translucent inks.*

OPPOSITE: *The Eskimo shaman enters a trance, and during his dance he is transported to the moon and to Sedna.*

TIRAI

Written, directed, and designed by Julie Taymor

Produced in Java, Sumatra, and Bali, 1978–79

New version produced at La MaMa Etc., Inc., New York City, 1981

Cowritten by Jon Lipsky

Sets by Jun Maeda

Costumes by Gabrielle Berry

T irai means "the curtain" in Bahasa Indonesia. In *topeng*, the traditional mask theater of Bali, the curtain stands at the back of the performance space. The performers emerge through the far-away curtain, bringing the past into the present. In traditional Western theater, the curtain is at the front of the stage and opens to bring those present—the audience—into the past.

The play was conceived after I had been living and traveling in Indonesia for two years, and it was the first production of my newly formed theater troupe, Teatr Loh. I wanted to create a piece that was a reflection of my own experience in Indonesia, one that would explore cultural identity, taboo, and boundary lines, but I also wanted it to be the product of the theater company's exploration into these themes. It was important that the perspective be from many points of view, and considering that Teatr Loh was composed of traditional and modern performers from East and West Java, Bali, France, Germany, and America, and included Hindus, Muslims, Jews, Christians, and atheists, this multifaceted perspective came quite naturally. Not since my work with Herbert Blau had I worked on a theater piece in this collaborative manner. While *Way of Snow* had been entirely my own creation, I was eager to invest in the group process once again, especially in such a direct and challenging context.

Tirai, set in Bali, tells the story of a family of mask dancers who are on their way to a ceremony that includes the initiation rite of their teenage son, Dia. Dia has one foot in the inherited world and one in the world of open opportunity. He wants to follow through with the traditions of his family and village, becoming a responsible member of the community, but at the same time he has been exposed to the personal autonomy of modern city life. En route to the ceremony Dia meets Zac, an American "gypsy," living by his wits, his wild-assed charm, and self-assurance. His unlikely companion is Ans, a Dutch geologist who has just returned to Bali, her birthplace, to study the active volcano at Batur. The ceremony is in Trunyan, a village near Batur, and Ans and Zac decide to attend. The story culminates with Dia's disastrous attempt to incorporate what he thinks is the best of both worlds into his own rite of passage. The result

The "infinite walking to the forever ceremony" in Tirai, *performed in Bali in 1979.*

is that he falls into a no-man's-land, having rejected the xenophobic purity of his own culture and yet having no bearings or direction in the ocean of "every man for himself." Ans, who tries to reconcile her scientific approach to the volcano with the spiritual and mythic understanding of the traditional Balinese, also comes close to losing her way. She thought perhaps that she was returning home but finds out that being born in Bali, speaking the language, learning the customs will never make her Balinese. And Zac, who foolishly thought he knew how to tread all cultural waters, nearly loses his life in a head-on collision with anti-Western animosity.

The dominant image for the piece was that of the infinite walking to the forever ceremony: all white, a flock of geese, carrying their world on their heads —flowers and fire (the sacred spirit), babies and babies (ongoing life), a table of rice fields (sustenance), and an umbrella tree (society's shelter and law). I saw it on a trip I took across the rice paddies and up the steep mountain slopes to Bugbug. The pilgrimage of hundreds of people laden with everything essential to life—food, musical instruments, children, machetes, and so on—transcending time, person, and place as they came to rest on the mountain peak. The trees were filled with pigs.

Tirai was a blending of a linear dramatic story with surreal imagery that lifted the familiar into the world of dreams and trance states. Immediately after the opening image of the ceremonial walking, where everyone wore white masks and moved as one in a choral, slow, and stately pace, the masks came off, exposing the individual faces of the actors. Expanded time gave way to "normal" time, the actors began to speak their lines, and the idiosyncrasies of the various characters began to emerge, revealing the baser human emotions of curiosity, greed, envy, love. The juxtaposition of the sacred and profane in my work commenced at this juncture, in *Tirai*. I wanted the audience to recognize these characters as their own family. Once that connection was made, I knew that they would travel anywhere with us. There were three different approaches to the face in *Tirai*. The white masks were about a state of being, whereas the human face was about the individual. The character masks used by the family performing their mask-dance drama represented kings, demons, and clowns.

During the mask-dance drama, which the family performs as part of the ceremonial celebrations, Dia's father, who resents the presence of the foreigners and is suspicious of their influence on his son, chooses the tale that the family will perform that night, "The Emperor's New Clothes." (Surprisingly, this tale is known all over Asia and seemed to me thoroughly appropriate to function as a satire exorcising the fears of aggressive Westernization of Indonesia.) The actors utilize comic and colorful half-masks fashioned in the traditional style of Java and Bali, so the play-within-the-play starts out as a naive entertainment. Zac and Ans, like the rest of the audience, sit on the sidelines watching and enjoying. Upon the arrival of the weavers, however, Dia's father subverts the innocence by appropriating the faces of Ans and Zac. He places face masks representing the two foreigners on the dancers who are playing the weavers. Suddenly the tale takes on political resonance. The weavers, who came from over the seas

The white masks worn by the family in the opening scene of the ritual "infinite walking."

ABOVE: *The cave people.*

OPPOSITE TOP: *The walk to the initiation ceremony.*

OPPOSITE BOTTOM: *The family makes a prayer to bless Dia's initiation.*

with their fancy looms, that is, modern equipment, deceive the natives into believing the newly woven cloth is the best and most desirable. (Indonesia is known as a textile giant, so this fuels their burgeoning rancor toward the West.) In fact, the weavers have woven no cloth at all, but everyone, afraid to appear foolish, praises the fabric, which they can't actually see. The emperor is paraded out into the streets garbed in his "new clothes," and it is finally a little child who shouts out the truth that the king is naked. At this point in the family's version of the story, the weavers are caught and sentenced to death. Ans and Zac are horrified that they have been personally manipulated into the story and all hell breaks loose . . .

This twist in the performing of the tale brought it to the present in a provocative and dangerous way, as is the custom with a great deal of the comedy in traditional Indonesian theater. The stories may be old but it is all in the manner of the telling. Also in the fashion of the traditional theater, this section of *Tirai* was always improvised because the traditional actors in my troupe were not used to memorizing lines. To have to repeat the same text night after night was boring and difficult for them. Allowing one section of the play to be improvised kept them on their toes and kept a freshness to the production.

Six languages were spoken in *Tirai*—Indonesian, Javanese, Balinese, English, German, and Bahasa Bluduk-uwuk-uwuk. The latter, made-up language, used only during the play-within-the-play, was unintelligible on purpose. Because Bahasa Bluduk-uwuk-uwuk was in actuality Balinese and Javanese turned backwards, the audience could follow the meaning via the sound and had a wonderful time in newly appreciating its own language as music.

Ans (Julie Taymor) covering Zac (Fred Maire) in the final scene of Tirai *as performed in Indonesia.*

The family, masked, performs the play-within-the-play, "The Emperor's New Clothes."

BELOW: *Sita (Suarti) plays the drum for the demon of the volcano (I Nyoman Catra).*

RIGHT: *Zac (Bill Irwin) clowning around with Sita, his heartthrob, and the great Balinese musician and dalang (shadow puppeteer), I Nyoman Sumandhi, who plays the role of a tree.*

BELOW RIGHT: *The family of dancers rehearsing their play, unmasked.*

THE HAGGADAH

Conceived, directed, and composed by Elizabeth Swados
Sets, costumes, masks, and puppetry by Julie Taymor
Lighting by Arden Fingerhut
Produced for the New York Shakespeare Festival, 1980, 1981, 1982;
aired on PBS Television, 1981

Elizabeth Swados asked me to work with her in creating a theatrical event based on the Passover Seder, the annual Jewish ritual commemorating the Exodus of the Hebrews from Egypt. The notion of a pageant play appealed to me as I had recently returned from Indonesia, where most of the traditional theater was connected to religious ceremony while also functioning as entertainment. Joseph Papp was supportive of the idea that the work would be specifically linked to Passover and would potentially be a yearly spring event at the Public Theater.

There was no script when we started, but the concept began with the idea of one large family at the Seder table (the audience being an extension of this family) reading from the Haggadah and observing the details of the ritual, which would unfold from the table into visual and musical spectacle during the course of the symbolic meal. While Liz worked on her cantata with texts from the Old Testament, the poetry of Elie Wiesel and Yehudah Amichai, and spirituals, I worked as the designer of the sets, costumes, masks, and puppets. With Liz I also conceived whole scenes and choreographed the movement of the puppeteers and dancers. The epic nature of the story was a terrific challenge. Cecil B. DeMille had done it on a grand and flamboyant scale as realistically as possible in his movie *The Ten Commandments*. Now, in contrast, I would need to abstract the events into the elemental imagery of the theater; through its simplicity it would spark the imagination of the audience.

The space, Luesther Hall at the Public Theater, was the catalyst for the entire design. The room was long and narrow and the walls were lined with giant arches, five on each side and two at each end. Upon first entering the hall, I immediately imagined the Ten Commandments in the two end arches and the Ten Plagues appearing like stained-glass windows surrounding the audience in the arches on either long side. The Seder table, a mirror of the shape of the

Pharaoh's sorcerers, whose two-dimensional movements evoked Egyptian hieroglyphics.

OPPOSITE: *Mt. Sinai.*

hall, would be in the middle of the room, and the audience would be seated on bleachers behind both long sides of it.

Besides the banquet table, and the arches filled with shadow screens and scrim, the only other set pieces were Egypt and Mt. Sinai, at the opposite ends of the room. In searching to find an ideograph to represent Egypt, I landed on the notion of an upside-down pyramid, a perfect man-made shape that pierces the earth. It also doubled as a Jack-in-the-box for a serpentine Pharaoh. In polar contrast stood Mt. Sinai, an asymmetrical pyramid, a natural form whose pinnacle reaches up toward heaven. This mount supported the entire chorus, with light glowing through its open wood-slatting.

Having only the bodies of twenty singer-dancers, I created the "cast of thousands" by using puppets and masks encompassing every style imaginable. The Ten Plagues were giant colored Plexiglas shadow puppets that filled the ten arches, creating kinetic stained-glass windows—frogs, locusts, wild beasts, and rats wrapping around the spectators. The rabbis and their wives were life-size foam latex hand-and-rod puppets that popped up in the chairs around the table to discuss and argue over the meaning of the Talmud and how to bake the Seder meal. The Hebrew slaves were represented by masked dancers carrying five-foot pyramids on their backs. The pyramids appeared to be made of matzoh, one of the ritual foods on the table.

Also emanating from the table was the scene of the Parting of the Red Sea. The white tablecloth began to expand until it filled the entire playing area. As Moses, a ten-foot-tall masked figure, began to lead the escaping Hebrews through the sea, the cloth began to ripple like waves via the simple hand movements of the puppeteers at each of its corners. To represent the parting of the sea, the two sides of the cloth rose in front of the audience. Light shining into the funnel allowed them to see through the translucent fabric as the shadowy, liquid figures passed by. At the climax of the passage, the top of the upside-down pyramid popped open to reveal the Pharaoh—a giant cobra whose head emerged out of the box, followed by twenty running puppeteers holding large shields that formed the body of the serpent. On each shield was a carved relief of the armies of the Pharaoh. The sea now rose high over the head of the serpent, the fabric filled with air, and with one violent downward motion the performers were able to create a huge wave that caught the Pharaoh and armies, swallowing and sweeping them away.

This double event or layering is fundamental to the way I conceive as a designer and director. Pharaoh is a serpent *and* a procession of armies. A table-cloth is transformed into the Red Sea. Through the simple movement of a few performers, a banal object that appears to be only what it is metamorphoses into a symbolic and mythic event that resonates with history, drama, and danger. The fact that at one moment it was a white tablecloth, performing its literal function in a very straightforward way, and at the next it claimed to be the Parting of the Red Sea, operating only through suggestion, relying on the poetic partici-pation of the audience, is to me the very essence and prerogative of the theater.

The Hebrew slaves carrying the pyra-mids on their backs: one of Taymor's first designs for The Haggadah.

RIGHT: *A Plexiglas shadow puppet of a plague victim.*

BELOW: *The plague of "disease" was represented by shadow puppets of two animals in death throes.*

OPPOSITE, CLOCKWISE FROM TOP LEFT: *The Hebrews carried pyramids that appeared to be made of matzoh; Moses; the Rabbis.*

Taymor's designs for shadow-puppet plague victims and, opposite, a drawing of Moses, whose hair resembles the burning bush.

BLACK ELK LIVES

Written by Christopher Sergel, based on the novel *Black Elk Speaks*
by John Neihardt
Directed by Tom Brennan
Sets, masks, and puppetry by Julie Taymor
Costumes by David Murin
Lighting by William Armstrong
Produced at Entermedia Theater, New York City, 1981

The adaptation to the stage of the novel *Black Elk Speaks* was not an easy proposition. The challenge of the playwright was to marry the historical events with the hallucinatory visions of Black Elk, the great Native American spiritual leader. As is usual for a play in script form, the writing was heavy on literal events that could be enacted by human beings and light on the miraculous and surreal visions themselves. Too often writers are afraid to include images that they think are impossible to realize on the stage. Either they suppose that by visualizing or concretizing the dream imagery it becomes trivialized and earthbound, or they just think it cannot be done except in the literal, special-effect manner of film.

I was invited into the process very late in the game. The script was finished. So in addition to creating an environment that was a setting for the action, I attempted to devise a playing space for the intangibles of the piece that had not been written into the script. A circular range of tepees on a thrust stage served as a ritual space for the powwow and suggested a mountain range. The materials were simple—translucent painted canvas stretched on tall tree-poles. One large enclosed tepee occupied center stage; a fire lit it from within. Immobile, silhouetted shadows of warriors, horses, and buffalo glowed on the translucent walls —pictographs, the traditional Indian method of documenting historical events, painted on the hides of the tepees. Slowly the shadows moved as the story came to life. The tepee opened, revealing a huge drum, a platform for the players. The drum head rose up vertically to become a shadow-screen for dreams.

As in *Way of Snow* and *The Haggadah*, puppetry enabled us to tell a story that goes beyond human interaction to encompass nature and the supernatural. In this case, though shadow puppetry is not associated with Native American ritual theater, its elusiveness and mystery supported the ephemeral character of Black Elk's visions.

Masks for the vision dances.

OPPOSITE: *The set was a landscape of tepees that doubled as a mountain range. Black Elk (Manu Topou) stands at right.*

SAVAGES

Written by Christopher Hampton

Directed by Jackson Phippin

Music by Teiji Ito

Sets by Tony Straiges

Costumes by Lesley Skannal

Masks and puppetry by Julie Taymor

Lighting and projections by Donald Edmund Thomas

Produced at Center Stage, Baltimore, Maryland, 1982

A larger-than-life-size relief puppet of a Brazilian Indian. Only her arms were articulated, so they could rise slowly to her mouth in a sign of fear.

*S*avages, a play by Christopher Hampton, centers on the slaughter, both physical and spiritual, of the Brazilian Indians. Originally, I was asked to design the costumes for the various characters, which included British consulate officials, Marxist revolutionaries, missionaries, and the Indians. Within a week, though, my role changed significantly.

Because the painted naked body is the dress of the Brazilian Indians, costumes were a moot point for a good percentage of the characters. I asked the director, Jackson Phippin, how he intended casting those roles. We agreed that to cast brown-skinned actors, whether Native American, Hispanic, or black, seemed uncomfortably wrong, for two reasons. First, nudity on stage could obviously be distracting. Second, as the play was written, the Indians were mostly a nonspeaking presence. Though they are the focal point of the play, it is their rituals that are designed to be enacted on the stage, in counterpoint to the more conventional dialogue scenes of the other characters. This also was a sensitive issue for me. My experience with genuine ritual performance in Indonesia had enhanced my aversion to the exploitation of exotic rituals through their mimicry on the commercial stage. The director and I agreed that we needed to find another solution to the portrayal of the Brazilian Indians.

I suggested that we not use actors at all for these parts. Because the play is not written from the Indian point of view but, in fact, objectifies them as it tells the tale from the white perspective, I recommended that we truly objectify them by making them larger-than-life sculpted figures. I felt that their silent presence would be even stronger if their state of physical being and their state of mind were carved into fixed positions with extremely limited movement. Phippin approved of this concept, and I proceeded to design relief sculptures that floated in a black void above the earthly playing space: A six-foot face with a large feather pierced through its nostrils peered out from behind giant jungle

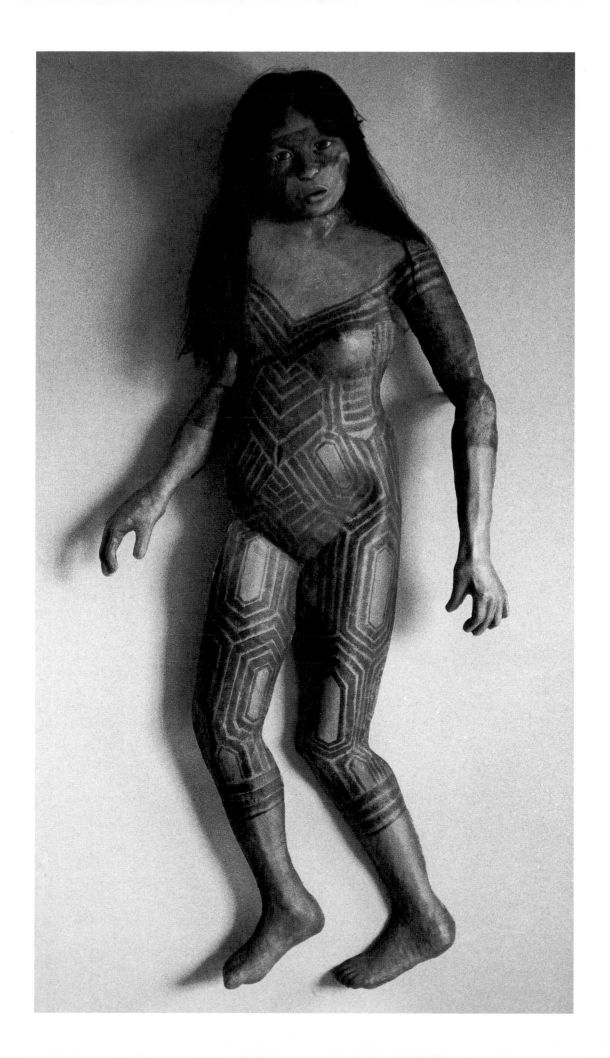

A Brazilian Indian (a four-foot mask) peered out from the giant jungle leaves.

OPPOSITE TOP: *The Indians in a ritual dance.*

OPPOSITE BOTTOM: *An Indian mother and her baby swung slowly in a hammock to the distant sound of Christian hymns.*

leaves to the sound of approaching helicopters. A young woman slowly raised her hand to her mouth—an ideograph of fear. A mother swung in a hemp hammock, her infant's fingers clutching her nipple while Christian hymns were sung in the distance.

The discipline of limitation was paramount in my designs for *Savages*. Ideographs had already become integral to my directing method, and I had always unconsciously been dealing with ideographs when designing masks. Ideographs are like Japanese brush paintings; one has to abstract the essence of the image into a few brushstrokes. Detail can be a distraction from the heart of the image. Already in choosing to design relief sculptures rather than fully dimensional figures I would be selecting the attitude of the characters as well as determining the point of view of the audience. Photographs of the Brazilian Indians from *National Geographic* were inspirations to this process. I felt like a voyeur gazing at the caught private moments of a distant people, their frank nudity a potent reminder of the vulnerability of their survival. I wanted the brief, haikulike moments in *Savages* to have that feel. And because the figures were much larger than life they became "close-ups," adding further to the notion of invaded privacy. In ideographing the gestures for each of the figures and eliminating extraneous movement, I looked for what was the most minimal action to express the essence of the moment in time.

THE KING STAG

Written by Carlo Gozzi; English translation by Albert Bermel

Directed by Andrei Serban

Music by Elliot Goldenthal

Sets by Michael H. Yeargan

Costumes, masks, puppetry, and choreography by Julie Taymor

Lighting by Jennifer Tipton

Produced at American Repertory Theater, Cambridge, Massachusetts, 1984;

toured in Europe, Japan, and the United States

Carlo Gozzi, the eighteenth-century playwright, wrote *The King Stag* in the tradition of the commedia dell'arte. This oriental fantasy is peopled with a host of stock commedia characters such as Pantalone, the old buffoon; Truffaldino, the whimsically clownish Harlequino; Deramo, the romantically noble king; Tartaglia, his wickedly evil prime minister; and others. In addition to the human elements is a wondrous array of animals and magical events. My task was to find a unifying style for all these elements that would blend Eastern and Western techniques and visual motifs.

We decided to use the traditional method of half-masks for the actors. This allowed the dialogue to be delivered and comprehended without obstruction. First, I made plaster casts of the actors' faces. These were the foundations upon which I sculpted the characters out of clay. The finished sculptures became molds, which were then covered in celastic, a cloth impregnated with plastic that, when dipped in the solvent acetone, becomes pliant. Like papier-mâché, these masks are extremely light and slightly flexible, which makes them bearable to wear. To finish the face, I designed makeup to be worn on the chin complementing the upper half-mask. Some of the characters' masks, however, had sculpted chin pieces that were separately strapped to the performers' faces, still allowing for the dialogue. A few of the actors wore piece masks, where only small portions of the face were covered, accenting the most important feature, such as a singularly long nose or high, balding forehead. In these cases, the unexposed portions allowed for terrific freedom of facial expression and were particularly appropriate for comic characters.

The challenging and sometimes disconcerting aspect of the mask process for actors is that the designer decides on the characters of the roles before the actors even get to rehearsal. It is absolutely critical that the actors have their masks from the first day of rehearsal, as they will inform the actors as to the

King Deramo (Thomas Derrah)
threatened by the evil prime minister,
Tartaglia (Richard Grusin).

Pantalone

Truffaldino

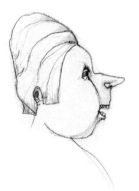

Cigolotti

OPPOSITE: *As two stags approach King Deramo, Tartaglia spots his opportunity to usurp power; Deramo proposes marriage to Angela (Diane D'Aquila).*

characters' idiosyncrasies as much as the dialogue will. And because the acting style is not naturalistic, the masks will also clue the actors as to their physical type of movement. The actors' bodies must complete the sculpture. The shape, color, and dominant features of the masks are the guide. This method of working from the outside in is more Eastern than Western and can be liberating to actors. For once, they are not necessarily typecast. Having their own faces hidden from view allows them to truly transform into other beings.

The costumes were designed to be as sculptured as the masks. They were not clothes that a character might choose to wear but were the core of the characters themselves. In some cases, as with Tartaglia, his cape held its bell-like structure thanks to rods sewn into the lining. Thus, when he would open his cape, taking hold of the two front poles, the effect was that of a bat spreading his threatening wings. The costume and mask demanded that he move in a certain way. At first the actor felt inhibited by the limiting nature of the costume. He could not kneel, sit, or put his hands on his hips without breaking, or wanting to break, the rods. These are the tension-filled moments that a designer "loves": Does the costume stay and the actor learn to use it? Or does one modify the design, making it comfortable to wear but ultimately lacking the edge of the original concept? In this case, through the encouragement of the director and myself, the actor discovered the power of his "wings," recognizing and embracing the essential physical vocabulary that was unique to him.

In Japanese Noh theater, the kimono demands that the wearer raise his or her arms only to a certain height. Beyond that the fabric will crease and weaken the image. The actor's talent lies in the quality of movement of the arms within that restrained scope.

The oriental aspect of the play allowed me to experiment with a variety of styles from all parts of Asia—Japan, the Philippines, Korea, Indonesia, Thailand, India, and China. The unifying factor was the blending and juxtaposing of the forms so that not one costume was recognizable as coming from a specific place. European details such as the white ruffled collars were thrown in to bridge the continents. To cohere the style further, every costume was made from white fabric and subsequently hand dyed, painted, or stenciled. Japanese block printed kites, with their glorious colors and patterns, were a source of inspiration.

I carried the notion of the kite into the various puppets designed for the play. Real paper bird kites from Taiwan, suspended from long bamboo poles, conquered the air space with marvelous simplicity. The stags were constructed out of stenciled silk stretched on shaped rattan frames whose moving parts were pulled by the strings of the visible puppeteer. The giant, fifteen-foot bear was also constructed out of rattan and parachute silk, which would fill with air, giving body to the animal. Light emanating from the milky Plexiglas floor illuminated the puppets' translucent fabric. These materials added a magical delicacy to the production. Again, as in *Savages*, I was looking to discover the minimal, elemental characteristics of a subject and its movement that, when the puppet was animated, would give it soul.

Angela, the love of King Deramo. Asian and European elements were combined in the design of the costumes.

Going a step further with the idea of translucency, I designed mirrored Plexiglas shadow puppets for the rest of the forest animals. This technique is as old as reflection itself. The ancient Chinese would bounce the sunlight off a carved mirror-stone to send messages great distances. In *The King Stag*, the puppeteers stood behind a large rear-projection screen holding the two-dimensional mirror puppets. Focused light bounced off the mirror and onto the screen, causing the figures to be white shadows rather than black ones. When the Plexiglas was bent slightly, the light image stretched and contorted on the screen, which caused it to look three dimensional, similar to holograms.

The only puppet of a human, and one of a totally different nature, was that of the bony old man, a life-size Bunraku-style puppet made of fiberglass and painted purple and white. Three puppeteers manipulated his body, but soon, as with the Bunraku from Japan, one forgot that the puppeteers were there at all. The movement was so lifelike in spirit that it became super-real and very moving. At one critical moment in the play, the heroine, Angela, performed by a flesh-and-blood actress, was asked to believe that trapped in the body of this old man was her husband, the young, handsome King Deramo. She gently carries the fragile figure in her arms. She sighs, sadly. He shudders with regret. The audience sees a pile of fiberglass limbs and yet suddenly, almost miraculously, through the physical and emotional interaction of this human being and this puppet, a heightened perception of humanity is engendered.

Air. Light. Breath.—Bringing to life the inanimate figure.

*Clarice (Lynn Chausow) is chastised
by her father, the evil Tartaglia.*

89

Durandarte
The King Stag
Julie Taymor

Truffaldino
The King Stag
Julie Taymor

Smeraldina
The King Stag
Julie Taymor

Brighella
The King Stag
Julie Taymor

Pantalone
The King Stag
Julie Taymor
1984

Tartaglia
The King Stag
Julie Taymor
'84

Leandro
The King Stag
Julie Taymor

Clarice
The King Stag
Julie Taymor

Deramo
The King Stag
Julie Taymor

Tartaglia takes over the body of the good King Deramo with a magic spell. The actor wore a mask that represented both characters.

OPPOSITE: *Taymor's color renderings for the costumes and masks.*

In the forest, a giant bear frightens the hunting party. Brighella (Harry S. Murphy) is on the ground, while Pantalone (Jeremy Geidt), in red, and Leandro (Christopher Moore) aim their guns.

OPPOSITE: *The curtain call featured the magician, Durandarte (Rodney Scott Hudson), in his parrot guise, standing over the body of Tartaglia.*

LIBERTY'S TAKEN

Book by David Suehsdorf and Julie Taymor

Music by Elliot Goldenthal

Lyrics by David Suehsdorf

Directed by Julie Taymor

Sets by G. W. Mercier

Costumes by Carol Oditz

Puppetry and masks by Julie Taymor

Choreography by Kimi Okada

Produced at the Castle Hill Festival, Ipswich, Massachusetts, 1985

L*iberty's Taken* is a tragicomic romance about the American Revolution and the men and women who fought it. This music-theater piece tells the love story of Jonathan Corncob, an apolitical scamp, and Susannah Wills, an idealistic patriot. Through Jonathan and Susannah are revealed two opposed but complementary strains of the American spirit: individualism ("Don't Tread on Me") and altruism ("Seek the Welfare of the City and You Shall Find Your Own"). As their rough and dark adventure unfolds, so too does a vast landscape of colorful characters and incidents in a theatrical underbelly of American fact and legend.

The plot was inspired by two main sources. The first is an eighteenth-century picaresque novel, *Adventures of Jonathan Corncob, Loyal American Refugee*. This anonymous work is reminiscent of Fielding's satire and operates on the conventions of coincidence, disguise, and mistaken identity. Its view of the Revolution is bawdy and irreverent. Second, *Liberty's Taken* draws on the biography of a historical figure, Deborah Sampson Gannett, an indentured servant who escaped bondage to fight in the Continental Army disguised as a man. *Liberty's* heroine, Susannah Wills, is modeled on Gannett. In addition to these sources, David Suehsdorf and I culled historical detail from letters, diaries, and folk art of the period. We made no attempt to give a history lesson but rather to tell a story that had not been heard. No George Washingtons, John Adamses, or midnight rides of Paul Revere. No famous battles, no tea, no Declarations, and no winners. Rather, a collage of aspirations and awful truths during a war for freedom.

Elliot Goldenthal's score required a vocal style that was unrefined and earthy. The urgency of the period was complemented by the rhythmically vital and nontraditional orchestration inspired by street music rather than the parlor music of the time. The instrumentation included hammer dulcimer, hurdy-gurdy, bagpipes, fiddle, brass, percussion, and keyboard.

Dinah Donewell, a Tory society lass who lustily gives Jonathan the pox.

Liberty's Taken *was performed out-doors. The main set-piece was a giant patchwork quilt whose squares could flip around to reveal other scenes. Here Jonathan (Todd Graff) milks a huge udder and dreams of leaving Virtue Falls.*

Mr. Bliss, the head of the Boston Committee of Safety, looking for traitors in Boston.

Susannah Wills (Donna Bullock) rides into Boston on horseback.

Two talking ship's figureheads, "The Havoc" and "Bouncing Sally," commiserate about their fate: though both were carved by the same carpenter, they now are on opposite sides of the war. The captains of the opposing navies are seated on the upstage ends of the seesaws, while a long shot of the entire battle is played out with shadow puppets in the background. A seasick Jonathan Corncob catches cannonballs.

Col. Pucie Brabber

Lt. Treen

The Jailer

Though epic in scale, with a "cast of hundreds," *Liberty's Taken* required the animating faculties of only a cast of twenty since we utilized puppetry in all its forms, both innovative and traditional—shadow puppets, rod, hand, and string puppets as well as full-, half-, and over-scale masks. Only the three main leads, Jonathan, Susannah, and Desire, were unmasked and fully dimensional characters. Juxtaposed with them was this highly stylized world of Dickensian characters, whose very essence of personality or purpose was stated in their extreme physical appearances, voices, and movements. This contrast enhanced and emphasized the humanity of our leads and helped the audience focus on their story in the midst of a swirling picaresque.

As in the music, American folk art, with its sophisticated naiveté, was a major inspiration to the design of the set as well as the puppets. Scenery popped up, unfolded, and was quite often anthropomorphic. The brothel was a twenty-foot-tall woman with the British flag over her head. Copulating shadow-puppets would be seen through parts of her body. A battle scene on the sea was enacted with two giant ship's figureheads seated on the downstage end of seesaws, while their captains, masked actors, rode up and down on the upstage ends. In the background, the long shot of the entire scene was played out in shadows.

On a superficial level American folk art appears benign, almost quaint. I took great pleasure in perverting these images when the darkness of a scene called for it. The fate of Captain Furnace's horse will serve as an example: It makes its first comedic appearance as a wooden hobbyhorse, at once a toy and a real animal. But by the final act, when the soldiers are starving, the only meat they can find is the captain's horse. And so they kill it, dismantling the thing piece by piece. The scene of starvation closes with the men champing on planks of wood.

The visuals of the production were as instrumental to telling the story of *Liberty's Taken* as were the book and music. Even materials and techniques were imbued with meaning and narrative power. The musical tells its tale not only from the perspective of the humans who inhabit it but also through the eyes of its animals, its weather vanes, hospital beds, patchwork quilts, windy seas, and frozen battlefields.

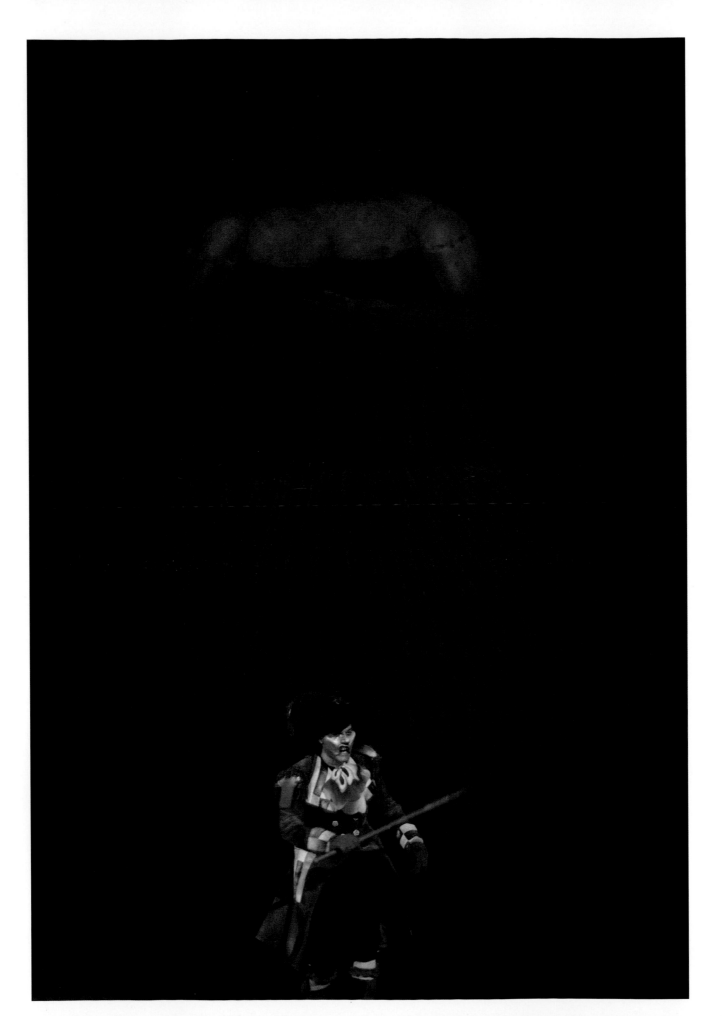

LEFT: *Desire Slawbunk (Leila Ivey) searching for her long-lost Jonathan.*

BELOW: *Susannah and Jonathan confront each other with accusations in the Rebel hospital in Peekskill.*

OPPOSITE: *The cockney pimp, Scatter Jackson (Paul Kandel), lures soldiers into the brothel, a twenty-foot-high woman with the British flag over her head.*

Lispenard
Brothel

Avery Dodge

The Minister

Maj. "Bloody" Grite

LEFT: *Dr. Pompidou of the Rebel hospital: "Live by the sword, die by the knife!"*

RIGHT: *Uncle Winters with his all-controlling mechanical hand.*

OPPOSITE: *Designs for the brothel and the copulating shadow puppets that appear in the torso of her giant body.*

THE TRANSPOSED HEADS

The Play:

Adapted by Sidney Goldfarb and Julie Taymor, based on the novella by Thomas Mann

Directed by Julie Taymor

Music by Yukio Tsuji and Masa Imamura

Sets by Atsushi Moriyasu

Costumes by Donna Zakowski

Puppetry and masks by Julie Taymor

Lighting by David N. Weiss

Lightscapes by Caterina Bertolotto

Produced at The Ark Theater, New York City, 1984

The Musical:

Book by Sidney Goldfarb

Music by Elliot Goldenthal

Lyrics by Sidney Goldfarb

Directed by Julie Taymor

Sets by Alexander Okun

Costumes by Carol Oditz

Puppetry and masks by Julie Taymor

Lighting by Pat Collins

Lightscapes by Caterina Bertolotto

Choreography by Margo Sappington, Julie Taymor, Rajika Puri, and Swati Gupta Bhise

Coproduced by American Music Theater Festival, Philadelphia, and Lincoln Center, New York City, 1986

Shridaman (Scott Burkholder) and Nanda (Byron Uttley) clasp hands in the ideograph of friendship. Balance is everything.

OPPOSITE: *Kali (Rajika Puri), the goddess of unbridled sex, blood, and blackness.*

A tale of a quintessential love triangle, *The Transposed Heads* tells the passionate and erotic story of two best friends in love with the same woman, Sita. Shridaman, her husband, is the "head"—all intellect and poetic yearning with not much of a body to speak of. Nanda, his best friend, is all "body"—physically beautiful yet earthbound in matters of the mind. Sita is torn between the two, not an uncommon dilemma in any world at any time. Wouldn't it be perfect if she could have the smart head on the sexy body? And so, in the manner of the best fairy tale or fantasy, an extraordinary event takes place via the divine intervention of Kali, goddess of unbridled sex, destruction, blood, and blackness. The two heads, which have been lopped off in acts of unbelievable self-sacrifice and desperation, are ceremoniously placed back on their bodies by Sita, only (perhaps by mistake?) she puts Shridaman's head on Nanda's body and vice versa . . .

This is just about where the original Indian legend winds down and Thomas Mann's adaptation takes off in a brilliant and darkly comic dissertation on the metaphysical issues of identity, maya (illusion), and the dichotomy of body and soul. What initially attracted me to the story was this unusual combination of philosophy with an accessible and tantalizing narrative that has it all—sex, violence, humor, and true love. In addition, though the story has wondrous supernatural events that demand inventive stagecraft, it is also a contained human tale requiring only four actors.

Though the play worked as a straight drama, two years after the original presentation we decided to fully musicalize it. The extreme events and the heightened emotionality of the piece were operatic, and I wanted a richer texture in the music to underscore the action. It was not an easy project to cast because it required actors who looked the part (physical appearance being a major theme) and could act, dance, and sing.

We maintained Mann's tone of voice, with its ironic edge and exquisite descriptions, in the production by including a narrator. Not only did the narrator's presence enhance the mythic quality of the story, but it also allowed us to have a neutral performer who could fill in the voices of the peripheral characters, such as the guru Kamadamana, while they were physically manifested by puppets. Though the narrator's voice was Mann's it came from the body of a woman. We costumed Rajika Puri (an Indian classical dancer and actress) in a man's formal swallowtail three-piece suit, her palms and the soles of her bare feet painted blood red, and her long black hair loose and wild to her waist. This androgynous presence danced precariously between Mann's controlled Germanic cool and Kali's terrifying, ravenous fire.

The piece opens in the black void of a smoking cremation ground. As the narrator scoops up their ashes into an urn, she introduces us to the two men: Behind her, in a wall of light, their bodies are formed. (This is a form of Black Theater, where the puppeteers, dressed in black, stand behind a wall of light and thus disappear. Only objects in the light are visible and can appear to float.) First the head of Shridaman appears, to the sound of a wistful bonsori flute.

Nanda and Shridaman in their ideographic poses in the kaleidoscope.

106

The rest of his body, piece by piece, floats in the light, finally taking position under the head. Simultaneously the body of Nanda is built, starting from the feet, accompanied by the earthy percussion of tablas. When they are fully formed, the two life-size sculpted relief puppets are replaced with fully dimensional live actors, whose movement carries them into the playing space. Once established as physical beings, each with his idiosyncratic rhythms and movement, they begin to speak. This incremental building of character brings into focus the differences between the two friends and sets up the theatrical conventions that are used in the rest of the piece—dance, song, puppetry, and so on.

The precise physical vocabulary of each man was the key to the later transposition of their heads. Though one would suppose life masks to be the answer to the technical challenge of this action, in fact they would have been quite inappropriate. The personality of each character was totally dependent on speech, song, and facial expression. The solution was to exchange bodies rather than heads. Each actor took on not only the costume of the other (Shridaman wore a bodysuit of Nanda muscles, while Nanda's body wore Shridaman's clothes) but also his entire way of moving.

In the musical version, the set consisted of a large triangular kaleidoscope. Alexander Okun in effect abstracted the play to its essence in physicalizing the love triangle. In that the play explores the concept of illusion, the mirror walls were a perfect surface with which to beguile and elude. Hand-painted projections of Indian miniature landscapes (outer place) and Tantric art (inner place) fragmented into mandala patterns and then dissolved like quicksilver into washes of pure color, or white or black emptiness.

Sita (Yamil Borges) tries to place the heads back on the bodies of her husband and his best friend.

OPPOSITE: *Kali dances maniacally as Sita makes her way back to Nanda.*

Kali/the narrator chastises Sita for her infidelity.

OPPOSITE TOP: *Kamada-mana, the ascetic, leaping in ecstasy as he describes the pitfalls of erotic love to Nanda, Sita, and Shrida-man.*

OPPOSITE BOTTOM: *Nanda and Shridaman fight over who is the husband of Sita once their heads have been transposed.*

The wedding of Sita and Shridaman.

OPPOSITE: Sita plays with her young son, Andhaka. The actress
manipulates the puppet herself.

113

THE TEMPEST

Written by William Shakespeare

Directed by Julie Taymor

Music by Elliot Goldenthal

Sets and costumes by G. W. Mercier

Puppetry and masks by Julie Taymor

Lighting by Francis Aronson

Lightscapes by Caterina Bertolotto

Produced by Theatre for a New Audience at CSC (Classic Stage Company),
New York City, 1986; Shakespeare Festival Theater, Stratford, Connecticut, 1987;
aired on PBS Television, "Behind the Scenes," 1993–94

I created a prologue. The house lights are up as the audience enters. Watching their approach, Prospero, like a caged tiger, paces in a circle, his long staff digging a path into the black sand. He has been exiled twelve years, on this island, waiting. At the top of the steep incline, the silhouette of a young girl, Miranda, can be seen against the white horizon. She is building a sand castle. As the last audience member sits down, Prospero suddenly turns upstage, his eyes riveted on a small white ship sailing across the horizon toward Miranda, his daughter. Prospero motions with his staff, and as the house lights dim, two figures in black carrying two black garden watering cans run on-stage. One comes to Prospero, who stands in the middle of his circle, which is now delineated by light. The other runs to Miranda. They both begin to pour water from their cans. Ceremoniously Prospero cups his hands to receive the water, while Miranda watches the water descend upon her sand castle. By a simple shift of focus, the light illuminating the entire action now illuminates only the falling water; it is raining. Prospero washes his hands and face with the rain in ritual preparation for the events to come. Miranda watches in dismay as the rainfall washes away her beautiful castle. The ship has by now sailed so close to Miranda that it appears to graze her shoulder. Prospero runs to the top of the hill, raises his staff high in the air, and with a violent gesture calls forth the tempest . . .

This prologue to my production of *The Tempest* sets forth the principals of Prospero's theater. He is the master puppeteer, the stage director of the events to take place. Prospero's tool is light: consciousness, introspection, understanding.

Ariel (Louise Smith) sets the ship on fire as Prospero (Robert Stattel) ignites the opening tempest.

OPPOSITE: *Prospero and Ariel.*

Called forth by Prospero, Caliban (Peter Callendar) emerges from the black sand. "This island's mine!" he rages.

OPPOSITE: *Prospero recounts to Miranda (Roxanne Caballero) the story of their arrival to the island.*

Prospero rips the head representing Ariel off the performer's hand in an angry display of domination. The actress, in black, is paralyzed and resembles a bare tree-stump.

It is technical and illusory. In one simple shift of light the audience sees the banal watering cans disappear, replaced by a vision of a natural event that appears to be propelled by no one. Scale shifts, and a "small watering" transforms into a "large rain." This exposing of the artifice will be a convention throughout the production, and the figures in black will function as Prospero's assistants.

Miranda's sand castle, introduced in the prologue, expresses a major theme of the play: the conflict between nature and nurture. One of the first images I had for the set was of a giant sand castle that would disintegrate slowly throughout the performance; an ideograph of nature conquering nurture, or civilization. When G. W. Mercier, the set designer, concluded that this was a bit much for the stagehands to handle each night, he came upon a simpler and more evocative concept for the set—an incline covered with black sand, invoking volcanic ash, and a blank white cyclorama that could be a tabula rasa for Prospero's imaginative powers. With the use of three-dimensional kinetic projections of light, the space could be transformed into a murky swamp, a labyrinthine forest, or a field of stars, and in a blink of the eye return to the barren black sand hill. Light as scenery reflects the interior landscapes of the mind while suggesting the exterior settings.

The prologue gives birth to the tempest, which is where Shakespeare's script begins. On a cue from Prospero, a large white sail suspended from a wooden mast unfurls from the flies. It billows wildly as Prospero's assistants try to secure it. In the center of the sail is the dark shadow of the ship (a metal shadow-puppet lit by a flame), tossing and turning, growing monstrous and miniature in size. This is a long shot of the storm-tossed ship. In front of the sail is a close-up of the same scene, in which the ship's voyagers— the king, his son, his courtiers, and the boatswain, who holds the wheel—struggle to stay on their feet. Each character, save the boatswain, is flung to his knees, humbled by the power of the tempest. This ideographic movement contains the essence of the scene, which maintains that only the captain of the ship is king in light of nature's wrath. At the climax of the storm, the sail is ripped from the mast and, like a huge wave, sweeps the voyagers away. Only the metal puppet of the ship remains on stage, its sails on fire and held high by one of Prospero's assistants.

Although I had done ideographic work with actors before, with Shakespeare it was critical that any physicalization of the text be bound by the rhythm and musicality of the language. I was interested in seeing how far an actor could heighten a character through physicalization—using physical expression to reveal a psychological situation. At the same time, I knew the text had to be spoken in such a way that it was natural and the sense could be understood. It was a constant balancing act for the actors to blend these two approaches.

The costumes for the production divided the characters into four categories: natural, supernatural, court, and clown. The degree of stylization depended on the character's range of expression. The costumes for Prospero, Miranda, and

"Ca Ca Caliban! Find a new master, get a new man!" Avery Brooks as Caliban.

With the help of Ariel, Prospero sets wild dogs on the foolish clowns—Stephano and Trinculo—and Caliban.

OPPOSITE TOP: *Caliban thinks the clowns (Reggie Montgomery and Kelly Walters) have come from the moon.*

OPPOSITE BOTTOM: *"An insubstantial pageant": Prospero has conjured up the goddesses Juno and Ceres to celebrate the betrothal of Miranda to Ferdinand.*

Ferdinand, who were the most fully fleshed out three-dimensional characters, were timeless, simple, and the most natural. Their costumes were off-white and earth toned, and the actors' faces were free of stage makeup. The court, on the contrary, was specifically dressed in Elizabethan style, each character a separate intense color that epitomized his or her position and personality. These characters were more two dimensional as written, so their faces were made up in the Kabuki style, which also demanded that their movement correspond. The clowns, Stephano and Trinculo, grotesque mirrors of the court, wore half-masks in the manner of the commedia dell'arte, which pushed the stylization even further. The fantastic visions conjured up by Prospero, such as Juno, Ceres, and the wild dogs, were puppets of two-dimensional shapes, light, and projection, thus carrying the stylization and nonhuman element to the ultimate extreme. This brings us to the two crucial characters in the play that most challenge a director's conception, Caliban and Ariel.

Caliban is described as a foul smelling, fishlike monster, less than human, the bastard of an evil "witch," and guilty of the near rape of Miranda. He may also be perceived as simply a native of this remote island, and the above description a product of the prejudicial point of view of the Europeans who have come to inhabit it, in particular Prospero, who now governs the island and Caliban as his own. Colonialization and abuse of power are dominant subjects of Shakespeare's text, and I chose to emphasize them in conceiving Caliban.

I took as my cue a line of Caliban's to Prospero in their first scene together, "For I am all the subjects that you have, / Which first was mine own king; and here you sty me / in this hard rock, whiles you do keep from me / the rest o' th' island." The image of a prison of hard rock stuck in my mind, and I was reminded of the masks of the Mud Men of New Guinea. I designed a similar primitive, rocklike head for Caliban, with only two eye holes, a mouth hole, and two ear holes for detail. It was a total dehumanization of the character. His personality was obliterated by the enforced masking of his face. In other words, he was only a "monster" as a by-product of how he was perceived and treated by his master, Prospero. The rest of the actor's nude body was coated with cracked blue-black clay, which gave the impression of parched earth. His body was beautiful, muscular, and athletic, representing the island through the powerful movement of its wild animals.

For the first third of the play Caliban is masked, but when he thinks he has been liberated by the clowns, a transformation occurs. In drunken exaltation, Caliban splits open his rock head with one of the logs he has been carrying for Prospero. As in a birth, his human face is finally revealed. Collecting the shattered fragments of his former head, he ties them to his waistband, to wear as totems of his enslavement throughout the play. While kneeling at the feet of Prospero, in their last interaction, Caliban takes a piece of the rock mask and humbly places it on his face. Prospero gently removes the totem, forever.

Ariel, the spiritual representation of human emotion, vulnerability, and compassion, is also Prospero's stage manager and muse. How does an actor play pure spirit, beyond male or female, appearing and disappearing on command, defying gravity, able to change shape and size, yet able to move the audience to laughter or tears? I knew that I wanted to use some form of puppetry to portray Ariel, but I was searching for the simplest and least encumbered technique. Then I rediscovered the power and flexibility of the disembodied mask. In Bali, in order to determine the personality of his or her mask, a dancer will first hold the mask in hand and with the littlest flick of the wrist cause it to come alive. This was the solution for Ariel. An actress dressed in the black garb of Prospero's assistants, her face hidden from view as in Bunraku puppetry, would manipulate a sculpted head with her right hand. The face of Ariel was androgynous and non-characterological, in the manner of the Eskimo and African spirit masks. It was a hard form with no moving parts, and I wanted to add the sense of air to the figure. I attached a long tail of translucent white silk that would delicately float with every movement of the head. Added to the image of the disembodied head was the disembodied left hand of the performer, wearing a glove in the same pearlescent white color, its fingers extended by a few inches. The hand acting with the head was able to express every emotion needed and by virtue of its simplicity was, ironically, even more poignant than had Ariel been truly human.

As when Caliban splits open his rock mask, Ariel too goes through a transformation on her liberation from Prospero in the final scene of the play: The sculpted head rests on the ground at Prospero's feet while the performer kneels, her own hidden face bowed. Prospero gently removes the black hood covering the performer and for the first time her face is revealed. She rises, acknowledging the stage and the theater, and, with exalted abandon, exits Prospero's domain, running through the audience and out of the theater.

As Prospero breaks his staff, the house lights go up. His power has been revealed and released.

Prospero draws a magic circle to trap his enemies.

Prospero with his magic staff and mantel controls the elements.

THE TAMING OF THE SHREW

Written by William Shakespeare

Directed by Julie Taymor

Music by Elliot Goldenthal

Sets by G. W. Mercier

Costumes by Catherine Zuber

Lighting by Beverly Emmons

Produced at Theatre for a New Audience, New York City, and in Beverly, Massachusetts, 1988

First of all I didn't cut the Sly prologue. A lot of directors do because it seems peripheral and unnecessary. But for me this play intentionally operates for two or three different audiences at the same time: those who, like the slobbery, lecherous, and drunken Sly, see it as a robust, sexy comedy where the "bitch" learns her lesson, and those who see it as a tale of the trials and tribulations of love and monogamy, where "the measure of love is how much you are willing to give up." Then there is the audience who writes it off as a dated, misogynist tract. I pity that audience. I am with those who adore Kate and her sharp and brilliant tongue and cannot possibly imagine that Shakespeare would give her all that great language, wit, and character if he did not love and respect her also. I say he put the Sly scene in to seduce, mislead, and cajole his groundling audience. If they want to be entertained as Sly is, then so be it. But if they wish to see a subtler tale, they need only observe very closely the love that blossoms between Kate and Petruchio.

Half of the characters in *Shrew* are dominated by the bourgeois, petty society, concerned with flirtations and traditional male-female roles. The play is set in a Boschian-Brueghelian time, when a woman's options were limited. I asked the actors to create a "mask" for these characters without actually wearing one. Juxtaposed with this stylized world are Kate and Petruchio. These two characters were explored for their dimensions, their psychological complexity.

For me, that is the key to this play. Petruchio *is* a swaggering, sexy, "wild Jack," but he also operates like a psychiatrist trying to understand what makes Kate tick. Kate is worth the agony he goes through not because of the money she

Petruchio (Sam Tsoutsouvas) arrives in rags to wed his bride, Katherina (Sheila Dabney).

BELOW: *Paul Kandel as the tailor.*

RIGHT: *Grumio (Kelly Walters), Petruchio's servant, feeds his master's horse.*

OPPOSITE: *Katherina tortures her sister Bianca (Wendy Makkena) by tying her up.*

brings—he already has that, being married to her—but because he soon recognizes himself in her. She is his match, if she only appreciated it. He suffers physically and mentally as he tries to get through to her, to get past the barbed wires she has constructed around herself to keep out the fools and the sycophants. His task is not to break her, as many have interpreted it, but to tear down the defenses so that she can learn to love.

And what about the last speech, where Kate chides shrewish womanhood and humbly submits to placing her hand below her husband's foot to "do him ease"? In my production, Kate made that speech from on top of the banquet table, which gave her tremendous power. She attacked the speech with gusto, seriousness, and fun, never losing the opportunity for a dig at her uppity sister Bianca. The moment where she offered her hand to Petruchio's foot may have seemed to her father, her sister, her suitors, and Sly to indicate that she had truly been tamed, but for Petruchio and Kate it had a different meaning. As they locked eyes and he quickly took her hand in his, he understood that she had given him a gift. She was willing to play the tamed woman, much as it might hurt her pride, because she loved him. The gesture was grand and it moved him. It was a private moment as the two slowly waltzed about the periphery of the stage oblivious to those, players and audience alike, who don't really get it.

JUAN DARIEN:
A CARNIVAL MASS

Written by Julie Taymor and Elliot Goldenthal, based on the short story

by Horacio Quiroga

Directed by Julie Taymor

Music by Elliot Goldenthal

Sets and costumes by G. W. Mercier and Julie Taymor

Puppetry and masks by Julie Taymor

Lighting by Richard Nelson (1988 production); Debrah Dumas (1990)

Produced at St. Clement's Church, New York City, 1988 and 1990 ; at festivals in

Edinburgh, Lille, Montreal, and Jerusalem, and in San Francisco, 1990–91

Imagery and music are the principal storytellers of *Juan Darién*. Though the Latin Requiem Mass serves as the text, language does not motivate events. It is not necessary to understand the text literally but instead to appreciate its sound as music, and its theme as it parallels Quiroga's seemingly naive tale. It is a Passion play—thus, our subtitle, *A Carnival Mass*.

In this South American story of compassion and revenge, the dominant adversaries are the church and the jungle. The opening image ignites this theme: The deteriorating walls of a mission church are overtaken by giant jungle leaves, while the distant voices of a Latin chorus are drowned out by a buzzing fecundity, in the form of copulating dragonflies.

Understanding man's elemental fear of the jaguar was paramount to understanding the savagery in *Juan Darién*. In order to bring home this South American obsession with the enemy—the jaguar—Elliot Goldenthal and I created "Tiger Tales," a series of shadow-puppet interludes depicting the nasty battle between man and beast. These "anti-plays," bawdy, scatological sketches, also functioned to break the linear structure, interrupt the tension, and disgrace the elegance and near preciousness of the piece. The technique used was primitive shadow-puppetry: leather shadow-puppets were slapped up against a handheld muslin screen, lit by a torch, and accompanied by crude vocal utterances. The Tiger Tales were presented as sideshows by the play's master of ceremonies, Mr. Bones. A descendant of the Day of the Dead ritual in Mexico, Mr. Bones, half jaguar/

Mounted on poles, these twelve-by-four-foot banners functioned, when stationary, as the setting for the carnival, but when manipulated by the performers, this "corporate puppet" became the mob that pursues Juan.

half man, topped with a bowler hat, manipulated the action of the play as both trickster and god.

The vocal score of the Mass was sung in a nonrefined, earthy manner by an ensemble of six women, all mezzo-sopranos, one rough, gravel voiced baritone, and a boy soprano (Juan) capable of singing in a pure lyric voice as well as producing violent, even guttural sounds. The dark sound of the women's voices dominated the play. Though this vocal quality is associated with motherhood and nurturing, mourning and prayer, there was a flip-side to the voices that emerged when they participated in Juan's torture, burning, and retransformation. Turning strident, harpylike, their soulful prayers seemed distant, almost hypocritical.

The instrumentation consisted of violin, trumpet, tuba, marimba, an array of world percussion, pre-Columbian clay flutes, whistles, jaw harp, didgeridoo, conch shell, and electronic keyboards and piano. With this ensemble, Goldenthal orchestrated the worlds of the church, carnival, and rainforest.

The scenery of *Juan Darién* consisted of the jungle and the village. The jungle was comprised of five large frames covered with giant jungle leaves and

The teacher (Leonard Petit) points his accusatory finger at the unruly children in the walking schoolhouse. When he gets angry the pages of his "hair" flap wildly.

Mr. Bones (Leonard Petit), the master of ceremonies, half human/half jaguar, appears in the village to maniacally celebrate this day of the dead.

suspended from the ceiling. Like marionettes, they could be moved horizontally and vertically to create various environments. Hanging the frames low and on-end created the effect of a dense jungle, while suspending them horizontally below the lights created a canopy effect. The other major scenic piece, the village, was a hemisphere structure that could move about the stage. One side revealed a village in forced perspective, complete with miniature houses, roads, a school, a church, and a graveyard at the summit. At night, interior lights illuminated the houses, and small shadow-puppet scenes of men drinking, a couple making love, another couple fighting, and so on appeared behind walls and windows. When the village was turned around, we saw the interior of the mother's house, also in forced perspective, but life-size in scale.

The puppets and masked characters in *Juan Darién* represented a multitude of techniques: Bunraku, hand, shadow, rod, string, and relief-sculpture puppets as well as oversized masks and fabricated body parts. The teacher, for instance, was nine feet tall. His nose supported five pairs of spectacles. His hair was an open book, with pages that fluttered when he was angry; and his hand culminated in a foot-long, bony, pointing finger. The teacher's schoolroom was a Punch and Judy type of walking stage supported by three puppeteers manipulating six hand-puppets of raucous schoolchildren, including a small version of Juan.

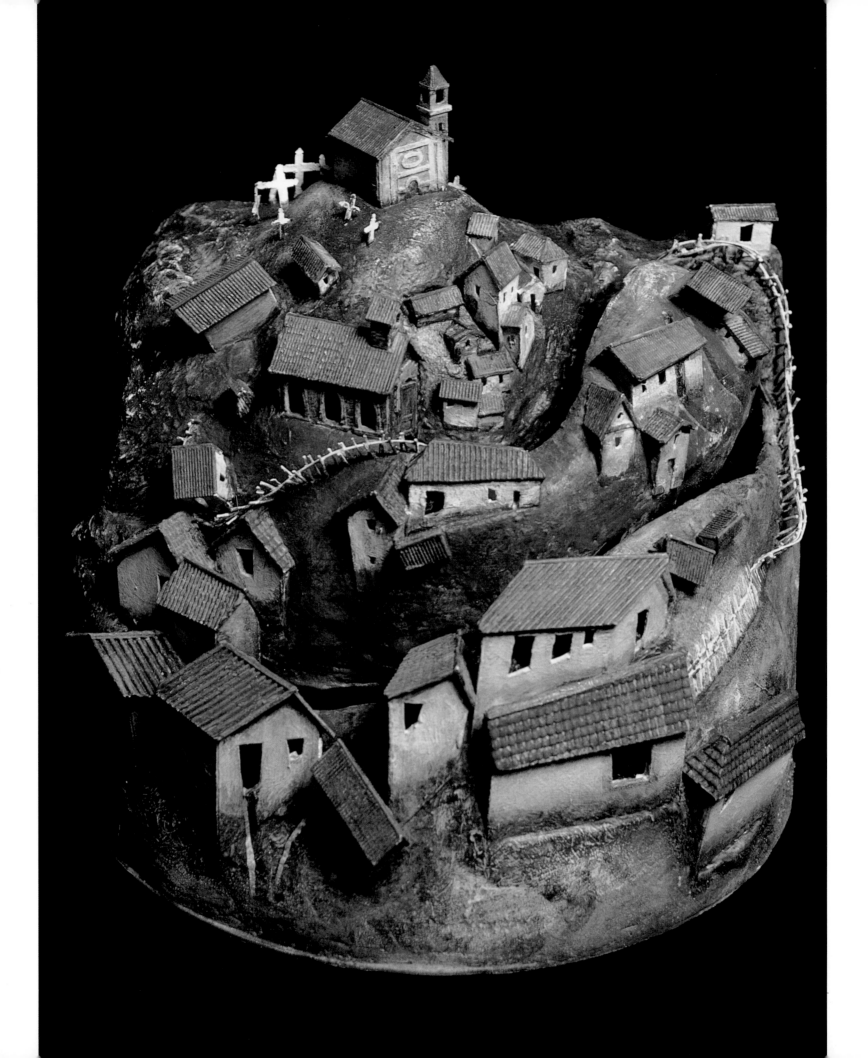

The hunter (Kris Batho) breaks into the mother's house looking for the jaguar, which she (Ariel Ashwell) hides under her shawl.

OPPOSITE: *A model of the set. At times the houses in the ten-foot-tall village lit up and revealed shadow-puppet scenes of the lives inside.*

A life-size Bunraku version of Juan sat alone at a desk in another part of the stage. In effect, we were seeing the interior and exterior experience of Juan at school in this dual-scale play.

Another example of the puppetry was the carnival crowd. Four giant banners, wildly painted with people and animals, were manipulated by puppeteers in such a way that they could function as the static perimeter of the fairground, a swirling calliope, or the labyrinthine mob that chases and ensnares Juan.

The juxtaposition of live actor and puppet was one of the key emotional and humanizing factors of the drama. The main character of Juan is transformed five times: at first he appears as a jaguar cub (rod-and-string puppet); next he becomes an infant (hand-manipulated doll); at age ten he changes into a four-foot-tall Bunraku puppet with realistic features; and upon the death of his mother he becomes a flesh-and-blood boy. The final transformation is pivotal to the theme and structure of *Juan Darién*. From this point on, Juan is the only human (unmasked) actor in the play. This theatrical choice heightens the irony during the *Dies Irae*, where Juan is accused of being a dangerous jaguar while everyone around him is not quite "human." The final transformation occurs when the child is burned alive on the Bengal lights (fireworks). He metamorphoses into a jaguar once again. But this time the child's face can be seen through the open mouth of the animal mask; his hands are covered by large paws; his naked torso has the blood-red stripes received during the whipping. This minimal transformation allows Juan to retain his humanness although his exterior is that of a ferocious beast.

At another point in the production, the revealing of the human face, the unmasking, has tremendous impact. Up until the middle of the *Dies Irae* the puppeteers have been anonymous, neutral figures clothed in black from head to toe. Upon the lighting of the torches that will engulf Juan in flames, the puppeteers remove the black veils, and for the first time we acknowledge them as people and as individuals. The abominable act of torture and murder belongs to human beings.

Upon her death, Juan's mother falls out of her mask and her human face is revealed (Thuli Dumakude and Lawrence A. Neals Jr.).

The plague has taken its toll in the village. Behind, a mother cradles her infant's coffin.

RIGHT: *Leather shadow-puppets are the performers in this "Tiger Tale."*

BELOW: *The barker (Matthew Kimbrough) chants as Señor Toledo (Kris Batho) throws knives at Mariposa, to the dismay of Juan.*

OPPOSITE: *Juan, suspected of being a jaguar, is burned alive on the fireworks scaffolding. In the flames he is transformed back into a beast.*

Sketches of the hunter.

OPPOSITE: *The mourning women of Juan's village.*

FOLLOWING PAGES: *Renderings of Señor Toledo, the schoolteacher, and the mother. Masks by Taymor, costumes designed with G.W. Mercier. At bottom, a relief sculpture of a plague victim.*

FOOL'S FIRE

Screenplay by Julie Taymor, based on the short story "Hop-Frog"
by Edgar Allan Poe

Directed by Julie Taymor

Original music by Elliott Goldenthal

Production design by G. W. Mercier

Costume and character design by Julie Taymor

Character technical design by Michael Curry

Director of Photography, Bobby Bukowski

Dance sequences by David Parsons

Executive Producers, American Playhouse and Rebo Studio, Line Producer,

Kerry Orent. Premiered at Sundance Film Festival, Park City, Utah; aired on

PBS Television, 1992

Fool's Fire is the world where theater meets cinema. It was inspired by those first masters of film, Lumière, Murnau, and Méliès, who not only through necessity but also through the love of a magical medium played with the world of reality by transforming it. Film is often used as a perfect device for recording what appears to be the natural world, but another challenge of the form is to exploit the tools at hand, to bend time and perspective, to alter our perceptions of the familiar to the point where we give our audience a totally fresh view of the subject. Edgar Allan Poe's short story "Hop-Frog" was a perfect vehicle to harness the highly visual and stylized directions I had been pursuing in the theater to a fantastical black comedy of revenge, replete with a fabulist plot, lush color, and grotesque characterizations.

Set in a medieval kingdom, the story tells of the captive dwarf, Hop-Frog, who is forced to play the court jester to a corpulent and oily king and his seven equally despicable ministers. Hop-Frog tolerates his miserable lot until one day another captive—the diminutive dancer, Trippetta— is brought to court to be a plaything of the king. Hop-Frog falls deeply in love with Trippetta and in order to avenge the cruel treatment that she receives at the lustful hands of the king and his ministers, he devises a wicked plot that culminates in their total destruction by fire.

In order to emphasize the point of view of the dwarf, the outsider, and the inhumane treatment he receives as the court toy, all the characters in the film—with

The king (Tom Hewitt).

144

the *exception* of Hop-Frog, his family, and Trippetta (all human actors)—were rendered using fantastical, Boschlike puppetry and masks. This choice allowed and in some ways forced the audience to identify with the tormented Hop-Frog and to accept and root for the ultimate retribution he delivers. His humanity and Trippetta's were underlined and heightened by the sheer denial of the human flesh and blood of the other characters. The moments when the shivering Hop-Frog was stripped naked in his barren garret, or Trippetta's finger bled from the tiny fragment of broken glass, had a visceral and psychological effect. The idea of the vulnerability of their flesh had extra impact and significance because it was confined to only these characters in the film. These two little people, so often used in the theater and cinema as special effects themselves, were deeply and painfully real.

In a parallel vein, clearly inanimate, mechanical dolls, sexual playthings of the lascivious lords, bore witness to the king's assault on Trippetta in the royal bathroom. Time was suspended, and the only reaction to Trippetta's fall came from the wooden heads of the dolls, which magically turned toward her, real tears springing from their painted eyes and streaming down their cracked and peeling faces.

As for all the other characters in *Fool's Fire*—the king, the ministers, and their ladies—the concept of utilizing puppets also seemed to support the bawdy, lyrical, scatological texture of their dialogue. It was a Rabelaisian menagerie, featuring a monarch and his cronies of huge proportions, lusty appetites, and cruel tastes. There was grand irony in that they were in reality puppets yet treated Hop-Frog as if he were less than human.

Taymor regarding the set of the banquet scene, built on an "insane rake."

*At the royal banquet, Hop-Frog
(Michael Anderson), under the table,
waits for a bone from the king.*

The king inspects Trippetta (Mireille Mossé), the gift given him by the Duke and Duchess of Sinisiri (Robert Dorfman and Joan MacIntosh), while Hop-Frog watches sadly.

The combination of High Definition TV with 35-millimeter film offered me marvelous potential in creating the surreal transitions and solving the demands of the dramatic scale and events of the grandiose finale. In HD, images are composited as they are shot. So, it was perfect for the scene in the ballroom, which appears, in the finished film, to be an immense hall filled with a hundred dancers. In fact, only ten live dancers were used for close shots in front of a full-scale portion of the ballroom set. For long or extremely high angle shots, these dancers were then matted together with another ninety miniature wooden mannequins into the interior of a model of the ballroom that was only twelve feet in diameter. Hop-Frog's final act of revenge required suspending the king and his seven ministers from the chandelier chain fifty feet in the air and then setting them on fire. Through the use of blue screen, miniatures, and matting techniques, we were able to layer our imagery, thus creating a vast and highly stylized landscape while fulfilling the dramatic needs of the script. The scenes that did not require manipulation were shot in 35-millimeter film because of its wonderful texture, depth, and flexibility of lenses. In the final process, the HD was transferred back to 35-millimeter, so it would blend with the rest of the film.

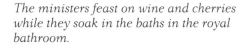

The ministers feast on wine and cherries while they soak in the baths in the royal bathroom.

Trippetta arrives at the court in a cage, dressed as a little bird.

OPPOSITE: *Hop-Frog, the court jester.*

151

ABOVE: *The last image of the film shows Hop-Frog manipulating a Pegasus puppet with small figures of himself and Trippetta escaping to freedom. For the first time in the story, Hop-Frog is huge, towering over the tiny world that no longer controls him.*

RIGHT: *The entrance of the guests to the king's masquerade ball. The dancers were designed to look like life-size wooden mannequins and were dressed in paper costumes.*

OPPOSITE: *The miniature ballroom. Wooden mannequins, also dressed in paper costumes, dance on a kaleidoscopic floor. This set was later matted together with the real dancers.*

LEFT: *Hop-Frog's father (Glenn Sturges) hides in the closet as the house is ransacked by marauders.*

BELOW: *Trippetta.*

OPPOSITE TOP: *Hop-Frog hesitates to drink the wine as the king has ordered.*

OPPOSITE BOTTOM: *Hop-Frog builds a chair for his love, Trippetta.*

*A portrait gallery of the king
and the ministers and ladies of the court.*

OEDIPUS REX

Composed by Igor Stravinsky

Libretto by Jean Cocteau

Live opera production and film directed by Julie Taymor

Conducted by Seiji Ozawa

Sets by George Tsypin

Costumes by Emi Wada

Masks and sculptures by Julie Taymor, technical design by Michael Curry

Choreography by Suzushi Hanayagi

Lighting by Jean Kalman

Makeup by Reiko Kruk

Director of Photography (film), Bobby Bukowski

Produced at the Saito Kinen Festival, Matsumoto, Japan, 1992

Film produced by Peter Gelb and Pat Jaffe, presented by Cami Video and NHK.

Premiered at Sundance Film Festival, Park City, Utah, 1993; aired on PBS Television and internationally

This production of Stravinsky's *Oedipus Rex* was a departure from the common oratorio form of presentation while, at the same time, it was inspired by the composer's original vision and intention. Stravinsky's decision to compose a work based on the play by Sophocles was prompted by his desire to find a universal plot, one so well known that there would be no need to elaborate its exposition. He stated, "I wished to leave the play, as a play, behind, thinking by this to distill the dramatic essence and to free myself for a greater degree of focus on a purely musical dramatization."

Where most productions of this opera stay within the minimalist guidelines created by the composer in his inherently nondramatic work, my challenge was to respond to Stravinsky's concepts while finding a complementary visual style that broadens the limitations of the minimalist vision. The static convention would be replaced with a theatrically dynamic spectacle that would support the music through abstract, elemental imagery.

Seeking to create a world that was both ancient and timeless, the designers and I were struck by the similarities between the early art of Japan and of the pre-Greek period from the isles of the Cyclades (3200–2200 B.C.). Cycladic and Haniwa sculpture were among the main inspirations for the imagery in our

Jessye Norman as Jocasta.

158

production. We were as much moved by time's corrosion of these ancient works as by their original beauty. The concept of deterioration, erosion, the corruption from within that is polluting the entire society, was the springboard for this archetypal drama of purification, and we made it an integral part of the design concept. George Tsypin's set consisted of a giant slatted wood deck floating above a pool of water. A canopy that was a mirror image of the deck was suspended overhead; a disc hanging in the center of the set evoked an eye—the disc as moon, Apollo's sun, and iris. The water waited to cleanse those who were polluted, and at the end of the opera the sky cried rain, washing the cracked clay from their bodies.

Beneath the facade of order there was chaos. Beneath the smooth stone and plaster surface, the infrastructure was rotting away. Its twigs and hay, arteries and veins were visible. Oedipus, the great king, was peeled apart like an onion until the truth was laid bare and the "monster" was revealed.

In staging *Oedipus Rex*, Stravinsky envisioned the use of masks for the principal singers so they would appear as living statues, emblems of the characters and states of being that they represent. The singers were not to relate to one another in a realistic manner but to sing their arias in presentational style, directly to the audience. Their movement was to be minimal to focus the tragedy not on Oedipus himself and the other individuals, but on the "fatal development" that, for Stravinsky, was the meaning of the play: "Crossroads are not personal but geometrical, and the geometry of tragedy, the inevitable intersecting of lines, is what concerned me." The red line was the recurring image throughout our production: the umbilical cord from which the infant Oedipus was suspended, the blood lines connecting parents and child that crossed to create the crossroads of taboo, the noose by which Jocasta hung herself, and finally the bloody tears that streamed from the pierced eyes of Oedipus.

This production followed the tradition of utilizing masks for its principal singers, though the manner of their use was quite unconventional. The masks were directly inspired by Cycladic sculptures of human figures, which embody the essence of human beings without the trappings of personality. Their faces have no eyes or mouth, which was perfect to represent the powerless portraits of the main players. By wearing the masks on top of their heads rather than in front of their faces, the singers were able to create the illusion of larger-than-life figures, monumental icons—as envisioned by Stravinsky. At the same time, with their faces exposed, the singers were free to express the emotional range of the music.

I chose to present two aspects of Oedipus: One was performed by a singer and one by a dancer. The dancer, whose mask was identical to the singer's, appeared on stage in fragmented visual flashbacks from the story of Oedipus. These tableaux vivants were not there to tell the whole tale but, as in the text, to distill the critical themes and images, the "monumental aspects of the story." Oedipus the dancer appeared as a living sculpture, the front part of his body from head to toe strapped into stone "armor." This, along with the cord from which he was suspended, intentionally gave the appearance of a puppet, a

OPPOSITE LEFT: *Red silk streams from the eyes of Oedipus the dancer (Min Tanaka), while Jocasta's hairpins remain firmly embedded in the mask worn by Oedipus the singer (Philip Langridge).*

OPPOSITE RIGHT: *The dancer Oedipus finally unites with the singer Oedipus for the final act—the piercing of his eyes. The moment is heightened by the blood-colored silk that drops, covering the entire back wall.*

symbolic image of a man caught and manipulated by exterior forces of fate. The back half of the dancer was left exposed, vulnerable, human. The naked flesh was bound, trapped in the frozen shell. By the end of the opera, the armor and mask would be shed and Oedipus would commit his final act, as a man, with all his fallibility, taking command of his own destiny.

Quotations of Stravinsky are taken from *Igor Stravinsky and Robert Craft, Dialogues,* University of California Press, Berkeley, 1982; and "A Classical Correspondence," *Opera News,* vol. 46, no. 8, pp. 16–18, 35–36.

Oedipus the dancer, on the disc, battles the sphinx as Oedipus the singer recounts the events.

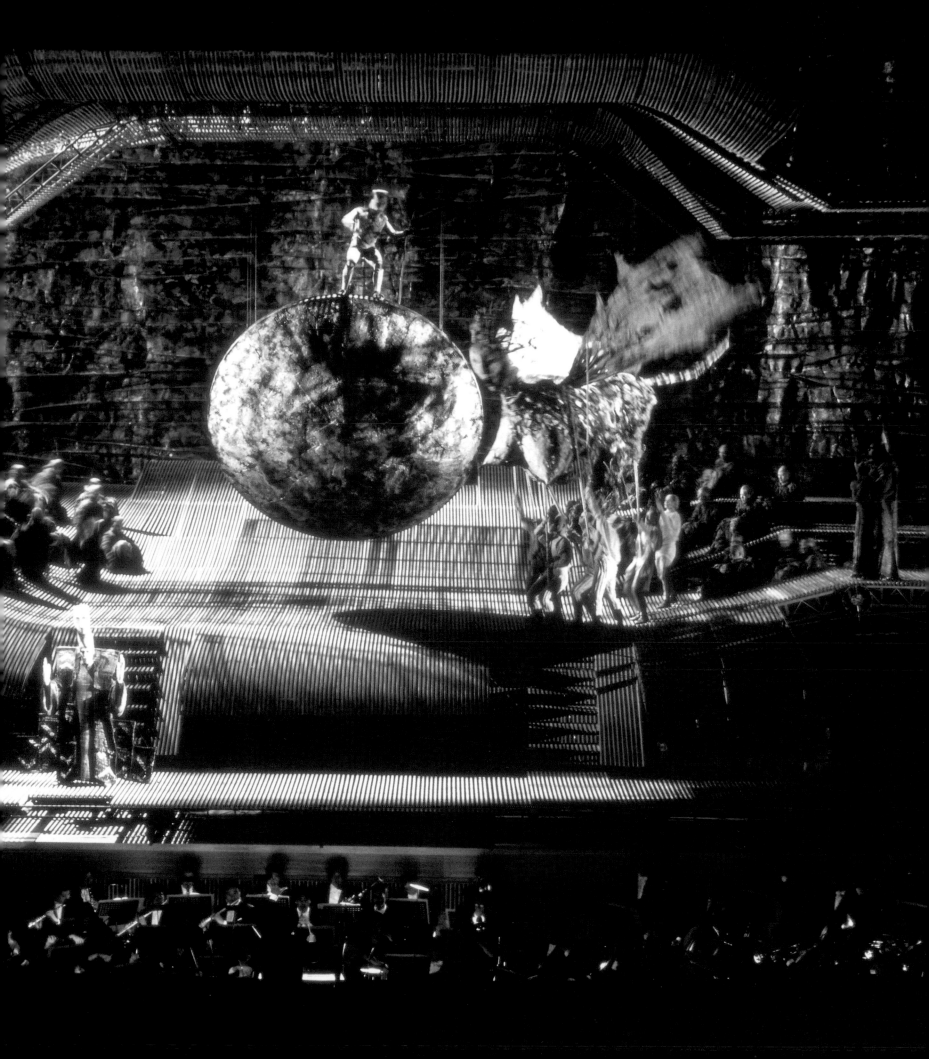

In the final scene Oedipus, blind and alone, walks through the water in the underworld as the rains begin to fall on the chorus, cleansing them.

OPPOSITE TOP: *Jocasta prepares to hang herself as her servants (Katerina Bakatsaki and Hisako Horikawa) express a silent wail.*

OPPOSITE BOTTOM: *Creon (Bryn Terfel) has just returned from the oracle of Apollo.*

RIGHT: *Oedipus recalls the events at the crossroads.*

BELOW: *Oedipus first appears hanging high above the stage from a red umbilical cord, surrounded by hungry vultures.*

OPPOSITE TOP: *The dancers, victims of the plague, await the arrival of Creon.*

OPPOSITE BOTTOM: *Half of the chorus members—forty men—stood, on the runways on either side of the proscenium, behind headless Cycladic sculptures. Their arms were crossed, as if in judgment on the events.*

The plague has struck Thebes.

OPPOSITE: *When Jocasta is hung, the head-crown disconnects from her body and flies into the air, suspended by the red silk noose.*

THE MAGIC FLUTE

Composed by Wolfgang Amadeus Mozart

Libretto by Emanuel Schikaneder

Directed by Julie Taymor

Conducted by Zubin Mehta

Sets by George Tsypin

Costumes by Julie Taymor

Masks and puppetry by Julie Taymor and Michael Curry

Lighting by Pat Collins

Projections by Wendall Harrington

Makeup by Reiko Kruk

Produced by the Maggio Musicale, Florence, Italy, 1993, and in Turin, 1994

T*he Magic Flute* is a metaphysical fairy tale that celebrates the rite of passage, both sexual and spiritual, of a young man, Tamino, and a young woman, Pamina. The challenge of staging this archetypal journey quest is to bring to light the dimensions and layers of the characters and events so that it is not a generic "fairy tale," distanced and prettified, but rather moves us on a visceral and immediate level. Though I intended to heed the enchanting, colorful nature of *The Magic Flute*, beloved by generations, I also sought to reveal the darker face, the one that is hidden in the innocent shell of the unruly libretto but apparent in the exquisite subtlety of the music.

In determining the world and tone of this production, I looked to the dominant themes of the score and the story as a springboard. The number three was the first one: the overture's three resounding opening chords, the key signature of three flats, the three boys, the three ladies, the pyramid, the holy trinity, and so on. The mystery of the numbers and the myriad symbols that permeate the opera are its lure and, as in the trials of Tamino, its game.

Even before delving into the Masonic references and mythic roots of the libretto, I became obsessed with the image of the triangular kaleidoscope as a perfect pyramidic vehicle to house both the exterior and inner landscapes of *The Magic Flute*. The simplicity and purity of the form, with its magical, transforming powers, would insure a *Flute* that could operate on a symbolic plane as well as an earthly, dramatic one. George Tsypin, the set designer, took off with the notion of architectural, geometric forms and designed three more mirror kaleidoscopes—a square and a small and large circle—to be used

The silhouette of Sarastro (Matthias Holle) in the center of the Tantric kaleidoscope. The priests hold lanterns.

One of the Three Ladies

Sarastro

The Speaker

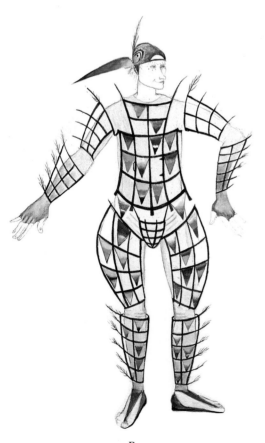

Pappageno

separately or in conjunction with each other for the various scenes. In the trials by fire and water, for example, the kaleidoscopes lined up one behind the other so that a Tantric mandala was formed. In the other trials, the kaleidoscopes were constantly shifting (moved by ten or more stagehands) in a dark void, creating an intangible, dangerous labyrinth. The front and rear projections that sometimes filled or surrounded the kaleidoscopes, designed by Wendall Harrington, were derived from Masonic, cabalistic, Tantric, and alchemical imagery and were rendered in either black-and-white detailed etchings or pure, saturated color. The decision to abstract the locales through these transitory projections accentuated the mystical dimension of the work, while certain projections of mountains, palace rooms, or gardens highlighted the literal map of the journey.

As the overture ends the curtain opens to a black void. Lights go up on Tamino asleep under a black-and-white checked blanket. (The black-and-white chessboard pattern is a dominant image in Masonic as well as Asian iconography, where good and evil exist only by the presence of each other.) A spiraling serpent appears over his head—fertility? infinity? wisdom? evil? It disappears. Under the blanket, a serpentine form slithers menacingly, its waves growing in size. Tamino sits bolt upright. The blanket is ripped off. The dream is reality. A huge serpent encompasses the void threatening Tamino . . .

As the costume, mask, and puppet designer as well as the director, I had to approach the characters in *The Magic Flute* in an all encompassing fashion.

The Queen of the Night

Monostatos

I wanted the singers to operate on a familiar, human level and a symbolic one—Pamina/water, Tamino/fire, Pappageno and his birds/air, Monostatos and his lustful passions/earth, the Queen of the Night/moon, Sarastro/the sun. Stylized gesture approaching dance was constantly juxtaposed with simple, natural actions. These subtle shifts in interpretation would magnify the emotional threads of the opera and highlight the humor. The following are a few examples.

The Queen of the Night first appears floating in the firmament, an exquisite white lunar moth whose twenty-foot wings contract and expand with her emotions. She is positioned high on an invisible platform. Behind her stand four dancers, also invisible, each holding a separate white wing of her costume. All four move in synch with her. Projected onto them are constantly dissolving dots of light, which cause the queen to appear as if made of stars and not of substance. The shift to woman/mother is signaled in the aria. At that point, the four wings lower, disappearing, leaving the queen alone, small, vulnerable, human. We see her as Tamino sees her, benevolent and moving. In her second appearance, in Act II, she loses control and the wings are violently dislocated from the singer's body, leaving her blood-red arms and spiderlike fingers exposed. The train of her virginal white dress also streams red. She now moves off her platform and freely takes the stage, her staccato movements fiercely angular and dominating. Her feet now firmly planted on earth, she is an all-too-human demoness. By her third incarnation, her wings are restored, her power intact, and her color thoroughly red.

Pamina

LEFT: *Pamina (Mariella Devia) lies on a bed of roses as Monostatos (Sergio Bertocchi) plans to rape her.*

BELOW: *Pappageno (Manfred Hemm) collecting his birds for the Queen of the Night.*

OPPOSITE: *Sarastro and the priests manipulate the lives of Pamina and Tamino (Deon van der Walt), miniature pawns on the giant chessboard. Masonic symbols surround the pyramid kaleidoscope.*

RIGHT: *Pappageno and his Pappagena (Lotte Leitner) singing of the many offspring they will have.*

BELOW: *The Queen of the Night (Sumi Jo) disowns Pamina as her daughter.*

OPPOSITE: *The three boys come to prevent Pamina from killing herself.*

The three boys fly by Pappageno suspended from bird kites. Sporting long white beards, these supernatural boys represent wisdom as well as youthful purity.

OPPOSITE: *Sarastro, center, listens to Tamino and Pamina sing of their love for each other, to the dismay of Monostatos.*

As Pappageno the birdcatcher is all about enslavement to one's belly, genitals, and heart, I wanted to play with the notion of a costume double-entendre. Instead of the usual bird getup I designed a pair of ordinary long johns; over these, strapped to his body, were rattan cages that functioned something like a baseball catcher's outfit—chest protector, gauntlets, and shin guards. Little swatches of colored silk were attached to the rattan and fluttered as he moved, suggesting feathers. This costume, as far as the character was concerned, was his bird-catching uniform. But the audience could see in it a man caged by his own needs and desires. Pappagena was designed similarly. When the two finally united in an orgy of sexual anticipation, each madly undressed the other, removing the cagelike corset, hoop-skirt, chest armor, and so on, right down to their unadorned underwear. Unencumbered, through love, they think that they are free. As they sang of the myriad children to be, the kaleidoscopic box they inhabited filled with birds (small silk puppets) while, one by one, bamboo poles were attached to the box, creating a larger cage to house the earthly family.

To create the animals, I took one step further the technique I had invented for *The King Stag*. In contrast to the too often too-cute stuffed animal costumes that accompany *Magic Flute* productions, I designed large kitelike beasts made of translucent fabric stretched over characters in shaped-aluminum frames with articulated moving parts. Manipulated by twenty dancers dressed in "invisible" black and backlit to glow, these delicate, minimalist animals possessed the same ethereal nature as the music.

178

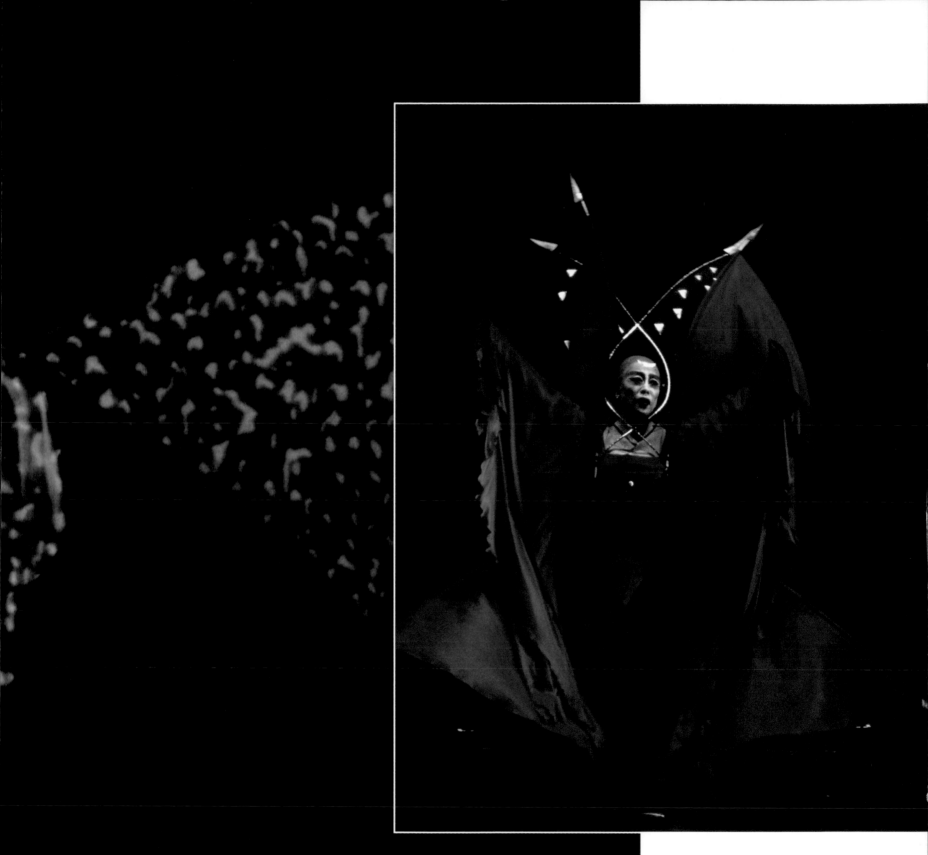

The Queen of the Night first appears like a white lunar moth floating in a galaxy of stars, and transforms into a red demoness in her last incarnation.

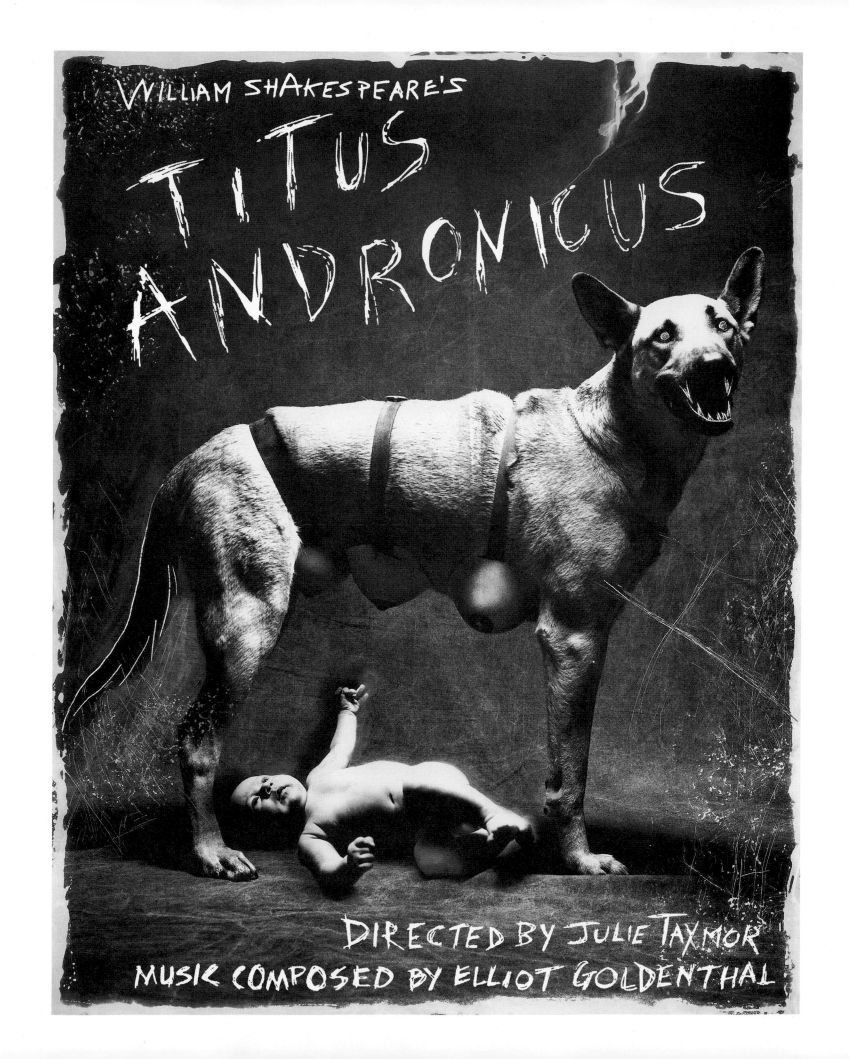

TITUS ANDRONICUS

Written by William Shakespeare

Directed by Julie Taymor

Music by Elliot Goldenthal

Sets by Derek McLane

Costumes by Constance Hoffman

Lighting by Donald Holder

Fight choreography by David Leong

Music Director, Richard Martinez

Produced by Theatre for a New Audience, New York City, 1994

For centuries, *Titus Andronicus* had been condemned as one of Shakespeare's worst plays although it was a very successful potboiler in his own day. Many have doubted its authenticity. Its heightened melodrama and obscene and ruthless violence juxtaposed with absurdist comedy seemed distasteful, over-the-top, and extremely difficult to stage. It is precisely those characteristics that fascinated me and convinced me that the play speaks directly to our times, when audiences feed daily on tabloid sex scandals, teenage gang rape, and the private details of a celebrity murder trial, when racism, ethnic cleansing, and genocide have almost ceased to shock by being so commonplace and seemingly inevitable. Our entertainment industry thrives on the graphic details of murders, rapes, and villainy, yet it is rare to find a film or play that not only reflects the dark events but also turns them inside out, probing and challenging our fundamental beliefs on morality and justice. For *Titus* is not a neat or safe play, where goodness triumphs over evil, but one in which, through relentless horror, the undeniable poetry of human tragedy emerges in full force, demanding that we examine the very root of violence and judge its various acts.

In preparing to direct *Titus*, I began an investigation of images of violence in sculpture, painting, and photography, from the elegant sculptures and paintings of the Rape of the Sabine Women to the grotesque and exquisitely moving world of photographer Joel Peter Witkin. The crucifixion itself, in all its gory details, has inspired artists and their spectators for centuries to respond to this image on every level of human experience, from the physical to the spiritual. The journey that Titus and almost every other character in the play takes demands that total experiencing, otherwise the drama becomes simply a series of horrific events, worthless trash, done up as camp or Grand Guignol.

The poster, conceived by Taymor, captured the tone of the production. It played with the mythic image of the Roman babes, Romulus and Remus, who were nursed at the teat of a wolf.

183

ABOVE AND OPPOSITE: *Titus (Robert Stattel) and his sons return to Rome, victorious in their war with the Goths.*

LEFT: *Titus's sons consecrate their swords in the fire before they sacrifice Alarbus (Samuel Baird), the eldest son of the Goth queen. The Goth prisoners look on in horror.*

My first question was, how does one portray the violent acts in *Titus*, which are so numerous and which encompass, rape, decapitation, mutilation, and sacrifice, in an era where movies are glutted with the most realistic and vivid depictions of such acts. In the theater, one usually chooses between realism and stylization, literalism or poetry, stage blood or red silk. For many years, people had suggested I direct this play knowing that many of my productions, from *Juan Darién* to *The Transposed Heads* to *Oedipus Rex* had dealt with extremely violent events through stylization. Now I had to decide if this approach was appropriate for *Titus*.

Stylizing an act of violence distances the audience from the event and thus potentially enables them to receive it on many different levels. Their minds and hearts are affected instead of their gut. Suggestion is often more harrowing than the real thing. In *Juan Darién*, for example, the boy is lashed; the perpetrator whips the floor as hard as he can, sound cracking, while the child is painted with stripes of red paint. It is mythic, larger than life. Though the audience feels the

In a ceremonial farewell, Titus pours sand into the boots representing his sons lost in battle.

pain, the visceral, gruesome reality of the act is superseded by its larger-than-life, mythic significance. On the other hand, a good display of stage blood spurting forth will engage their bodies, sending their adrenaline rushing. I wanted the audience to experience both reactions. I wanted them both inside and outside the events, reeling with the horror in their bellies and challenged with the dilemmas in their minds. I also wanted the audience to experience the danger and unease of not knowing what form the acts would take. Complacency as a result of familiarity is an enemy.

For example, the cutting off of Lavinia's hands takes place off-stage, and when she returns, her "stumps" are in fact scraggly twigs (lashed to her wrists over black gloves)—a poetic metamorphosis in the manner of Ovid. But when Aaron lops off Titus's hands with a jackknife, the gruesome action is done in full view. The pain, the scream, the mess of blood, the rags to stop the bleeding, all matter-of-fact and no fancy.

The decision to combine realism and stylization became a concept not only for the treatment of violence but also for the production as a whole, from design to choreography to actors' performances. In deciding on this approach, I took my cue from Shakespeare himself. The genius of his drama is that he juxtaposes very direct, simple, and visceral actions with immense poetic verbal imagery, overindulging in neither gratuitous action nor sentimental poeticizing. Within this very gritty drama there is a constant referencing to Latin and Greek mythology as well as to animal and elemental symbolism. We see the teeth of cruelty and then hear that, "Rome is but a wilderness of tigers. . . ." Lavinia, Titus's daughter, is often referred to as a doe, and her rape and mutilation have direct parallels in the story of Philomela in Ovid's *Metamorphosis*. These images became quite concrete in my mind and seemed crucial to the physical telling of the tale. As in *The Tempest*, I sought to theatricalize the rich imagery of Shakespeare's language. Verbal motifs would become visual ones. The image of Lavinia, the doe, being ravished by Chiron and Demetrius, at once the sons of Tamora and ferocious tigers, had to be realized.

I devised the concept of the "Penny Arcade Nightmares" (PANs) to portray the inner landscapes of the mind as affected by the external actions. These stylized, haikulike images appeared at various points throughout the play, counterpointing the realistic events in a dreamlike, surreal, and mythic manner. The "penny arcade," or sideshow, was heightened by Elliot Goldenthal's score, which played against the purity, elegance, and beauty of the imagery with a demonic, carnivalesque twist. These tableaux vivants were contained in floating gold frames and revealed by the drawing of tattered red velvet curtains. The images were further abstracted by their being positioned behind a translucent layer of plastic that was scarred with scratches and spattered and smudged with black ink, like a rotting old photograph.

The first PAN appeared at the end of Act I and revealed the floating body parts of Alarbus, the son of Tamora who was sacrificed by Titus in a Roman

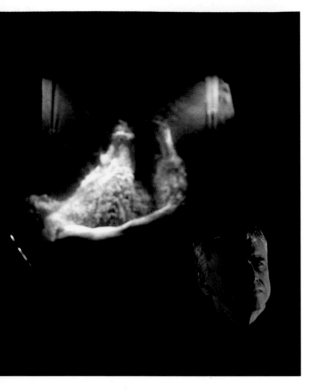

ABOVE: *In the third Penny Arcade Nightmare, Titus is visited by a vision of Mutius (Adam Stein), the son he has wrongly murdered. Half boy/half sacrificial lamb, this image occurs when Titus is pleading for the life of his two innocent but condemned sons. Though Mutius's death is not brought up again in the play after it takes place, it haunts Titus and underlies his pleas for mercy.*

RIGHT: *A PAN of Rape, Revenge, and Murder.*

OPPOSITE: *"Rome is but a wilderness of tigers. . . ." Lavinia (Miriam Healy-Louis), the "doe," is raped by Chiron (Jean Loup Wolfman) and Demetrius (Sebastian Roché), "tigers," in the second Penny Arcade Nightmare. The original concept included the effect of wind blowing up her petticoat, causing her to use her doe arms to keep the skirts down. The famous image of Marilyn Monroe holding her dress down over the subway grate seemed an apt modern iconic parallel to add to this scene of humiliation and rape. I was interested in exploiting our store of not only classical but also contemporary myths.*

ritual during the first scene of the play. Though Shakespeare does not portray the brutal act on-stage, allowing the audience to view the horror, I placed my first PAN at a point where seeming tranquility between the enemies, Titus and Tamora, had been established. They are the only people left on stage to "see" the image of the dismembered Alarbus. His sacrifice is the seminal event that motivates the acts of vengeance throughout the play.

The second PAN depicts the rape and mutilation of Lavinia by the sons of Tamora, Demetrius and Chiron. Once again, Shakespeare did not write this scene to be on stage, so my approach was not to be literal. To the strains of carny music gone mad, the curtain opens to reveal Lavinia stripped to her torn petticoat atop a truncated column. This ironic image conjures up references to such classical sculptures as the Venus de Milo, soon to be completed with truncated limbs and all. Her head is topped with the head of a doe while her arms are gloved with the doe's hooves. At her feet Demetrius and Chiron, ferocious "tigers," attack and ravish the doe/woman.

PAN number four started to break the convention of nonliteral imagery. A scheme concocted by the crafty and demonic Aaron results in the decapitated heads of Titus's two sons and Titus's own hand being sent back to him in scorn. At this point in the play, the violence has escalated to absurd and grotesque proportions. A cart is wheeled out, on top of which sits a gold frame with the now familiar red curtain. A messenger as carnival barker seats Titus and family before the mini-stage, preparing them for the entertainment. The curtain opens and they are assaulted by the sight of the two heads flowing in yellowish liquid in glass specimen jars and the amputated hand draped over a mound of black velvet. Unlike the other PANs, which were abstract or symbolic representations of an event or psychic state, this "still life" PAN is actually happening and signals the turn in the play where the nightmares are now reality and madness can be confused with sanity. Order has been replaced with chaos and the road to justice is paved with revenge.

By the fifth PAN Titus has been labeled mad by his enemies and friends alike. In a scene that refers to the classic image of David's painting of Marat, Titus soaks in his bathtub while writing decrees of vengeance with the blood from his wound. A loud knocking disturbs his contemplation, and to the distant strains of carnival music the gold frame and curtain enter Titus's space. At this point in the play, I wanted the audience to believe that what appears as the curtain opens is a figment of Titus's tortured mind.

Seated in front of a whirling wheel of Boschian demons sits the goddess Revenge. Her crown of daggers reminds us of the Statue of Liberty, while the black blindfold suggests Blind Justice. Where hands should be she wears two coned gauntlets. Her pendulous breasts form her shield and a plastic tube is attached to one of her nipples, feeding smoke into the mouth of Murder, who sports a tiger head as a hat. Above her right shoulder perches Rape, dressed only in a girl's training bra and panties and his head enveloped in the out-stretched wings of an owl. Masquerading in these wild costumes are Tamora and her guilty sons Demetrius and Chiron, who have come to torment Titus.

In the fourth PAN, Titus, with the severed head of one of his sons, vows vengeance on his enemies.

While framed, the controlled nightmare appears as if it is from Titus's point of view, but once the masqueraders step out of the frame, the vision becomes reality.

In the next-to-last scene in the play, Titus unmasks and kills Demetrius and Chiron. There is no frame to distance the action as he turns them upside-down, strapped to metal slabs that rise out of truncated classical columns, paralleling the image of Lavinia's rape. As Titus cuts their throats, Lavinia catches their blood in a basin. We learn of Titus's plan to bake the boys into pies that he will feed to their mother in the upcoming banquet scene. The proscenium curtain closes with a flourish, and the footlights illuminate the giant gold frame that surrounds the proscenium. Suddenly the entire play is a Penny Arcade Nightmare and Titus is the artist conceiving and delivering it. When the curtain reopens, it swags in the manner of the old-fashioned vaudeville stage, signaling the conscious presence of "theater," "entertainment!" in the events to come. Upstage, the familiar gold frame of the PANs appears and it has been transformed into a simple window in Titus's dining room. The red curtains are swagged open, an inner layer of white chiffon curtains is blown by a gentle breeze, and the only other subject in this PAN is a backdrop of beautiful blue sky: the window where Betty Crocker cools her pies. Birds chirping, the calm before the storm.

Titus "hallucinates" the PAN of Rape, Revenge, and Murder while in his tub.

Lavinia pleads for her life one last time to Tamora (Melinda Mullins) before Demetrius and Chiron rape and mutilate her.

ABOVE: *Lavinia, ravished, with her tongue cut out and her hands severed from her arms, is left abandoned on the pedestal. Her hands have been replaced with broken twigs.*

RIGHT: *Titus holds his daughter, Lavinia.*

OPPOSITE: *Tamora and her lover, Aaron the Moor (Harry Lennix), plot to kill Bassianus, the emperor's brother.*

The bloodbath that follows culminates in Titus's ultimate revenge, which leaves practically everyone dead.

On the first day of rehearsal, we read the play with the entire cast present. Then, for the next few days, we split the rehearsal between an exploration of the text and a totally freewheeling, improvisatory dissection of the themes of the play. I did not want people to isolate themselves into their characters too early. It was more important to establish an ensemble milieu where anything could occur and the actors would feel safe, especially in a play that is so intensely violent. Group and individual ideographs on themes of violence, power, ritual, godlessness, vengeance, and so on, as well as investigative interviews with each of the characters, summoned up a huge amount of potential material. Photographs, paintings, newspaper clippings were all fodder. As we continued to work on the play, certain scenes, speeches, textual images demanded that the actors continue to explore in an abstract, physical manner while discovering their characters. Certain moments in this process stand out to me:

The speech Marcus makes to Lavinia, his niece, on confronting her mutilation functions like an aria, where time and reality are suspended. If the actors continue to act in a naturalistic manner, the scene becomes absurd; why is he talking so much when she could just bleed to death? By placing the bloodied, ravished Lavinia on a truncated column while Marcus looks up at her from a distance, a physical metaphor was created that represented their entire life's relationship. She, the once-perfect goddess, is now a tree whose limbs have been lopped off, helpless, unable to get down from her pedestal. Marcus can only circle her from below. The space that separates them is palpable. As he speaks of her now and how she used to be, we do not question his lack of action but feel for his impotency, fear, and rage. When he finally takes her down off the pedestal and into his arms, the physical contact is startling and deeply emotional because it has been pointedly denied for so long.

In other scenes actors were asked to play like instrumentalists in a symphonic work rather than as soloists. Sometimes this meant an individual had to sublimate his or her character's needs in the interest of the larger scene as a whole. For example, because we had a limited number of actors we had to create the illusion of many guards attacking Titus's sons as they stole their sister out of the palace. The sons, as a unit, retreated backwards in a slow choral manner, thrusting their swords in staccato syncopation at the invisible attackers. One of the actors complained that his character would never move in that manner. I explained to him that we were not looking at his character, that this moment in the scene was about the whole event, not unlike a long shot in a film. Had each character moved as an individual, it would have diminished the dramatic, physical power of the action. These moments of group choreography only heightened, by juxtaposition, the more personal, naturalistic interactions that were the heart of the production.

While I was devising the notion of the PANs, Derek McLane, the set designer, and Constance Hoffman, the costume designer, collaborated with me in finding

His hand just cut off, Titus kneels in despairing unity with his daughter, while his brother Marcus (Michael Rudko) looks on in pity.

The nurse (Jean Barker) arrives with Tamora's infant to the hangout of Demetrius, Aaron, and Chiron.

OPPOSITE: *A seemingly mad Titus orders his kinsmen to send to the gods arrows wrapped in letters seeking justice.*

the appropriate context—time and place—for the play. Although Shakespeare was extremely selective in choosing the periods for his plays, I felt that this play in particular was palpably contemporary. More to the point, it felt both ancient and modern simultaneously. So McLane designed a flexible set that could either be an empty void or could evoke the various Roman settings. It consisted of ancient Roman columns that were black-and-white xeroxed photo blow-ups on stretched translucent plastic that could track in and out of the space. The back wall was occupied by a plastic cyc that was distressed and scarred with black ink. We were looking, as in the PANs, for a combination of stateliness, classical elegance, and a cheesy, theatrical crudeness, something that suggested the weight of history and conveyed impermanence. We limited our color palette to black, white, red, and blue—the colors of the veins below our skin. Another major scenic element was a Victorian, Roman-style bathtub that tripled as the public bath where the soldiers purified themselves, the pit in the forest, and Titus's bath. In addition, there was a 1950s chrome, red-topped kitchen table that served not only as what it literally was but also as a sacrificial altar and the final banquet table. This simple, banal piece of furniture was of major import for me. I wanted something familiar and ordinary to ground the events of the story, to bring them home.

Costumes were conceived to express personalities of people and the nature of events rather than to establish time. Titus progressed from ancient battle dress, completely black, to Eisenhower jacket, to a baggy gray sweater and loose-fitting corduroy pants, to a terrycloth robe, to, finally, his cook's outfit, all white. Tamora could have come out of Visconti's 1930s film *The Damned*, while Lavinia, "the jewel of Rome," was dressed like Grace Kelly. These references were not literal but suggestive, playing on archetypes.

I opened the production with an overture, a minute-long scene that would establish the tone of the play and also its point of view. Seated at the red kitchen-table is a thirteen-year-old boy, dressed in white t-shirt and black jeans, eating his supper. He wears a brown paper bag over his head, with eye and mouth holes cut out to form a mask. On the table in front of his plate are toy soldiers—Romans, Vikings, and GI Joes. The score begins with the comic sounds of TV violence—the Three Stooges, Popeye, Kung Fu movies, and such; the sound and music escalate, and the TV noise mutates to the real sounds of actual violence—a man beating a screaming woman, gunfire, ambulance sirens, bombs dropping, WAR. During this time the child begins innocently playing with his food and toys, but soon the action becomes ferociously violent as pieces fly, and like a mad god, he douses his victims with ketchup and mustard. When screaming sirens become unbearable, the frightened child covers his ears and crawls under the table to hide. This child is Young Lucius, Titus's grandchild, and now, as the story truly begins, he will play his part and witness the horror firsthand. The child becomes our other eyes, and the '50s kitchen gives way to the return from war of Roman soldiers in full battle armor.

The fact that the entire production was contained within a giant proscenium gold frame and red curtain, connecting it to the PANs and referring to the

Aaron tries to save his baby, while a Goth soldier stands guard.

vaudeville stages and revenge theatricals of old, was of primary importance to my staging of *Titus*. This traditional framing device signals to the audience that they are watching an entertainment and their awareness of this relationship to the play will not change. The tension between the audience as objective observers and subjective participants in the drama is very much built into Shakespeare's script. Not only the asides to the audience but also the irreverent juxtaposition of lowbrow humor with delicate and heart-wrenching introspection demands a constant shifting of audience involvement in the work. This play is as much about how the audience experiences violence as entertainment as it is about the tragedy of the endless cycle of violence itself.

Lavinia collects the blood from Chiron and Demetrius for a recipe for revenge.

OPPOSITE: *Titus embraces his daughter and then breaks her neck, killing her.*

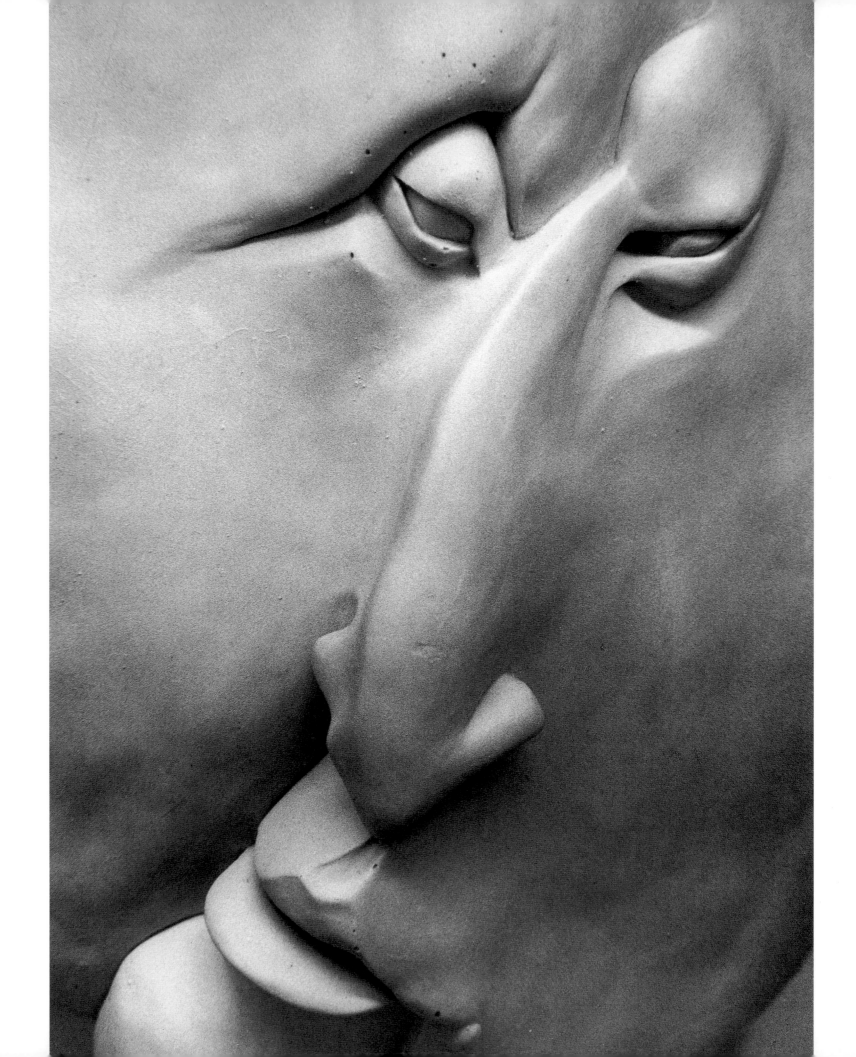

ACKNOWLEDGMENTS

Seeing Julie Taymor's work over fifteen years has been one of the great pleasures and influences in my theater life. I had long been intrigued by non-Western forms, but Julie's early shows sent me back to Asia to explore more seriously. And she has fanned my passion for theater that transcends the limitations of found (i.e., human) actors. My previous writing about Julie's work (in *American Theatre*, *The New York Times*, *The Wall Street Journal*, and *The Village Voice*) has always been deeply admiring, but not uncritical. I feel flattered and privileged that she asked me to do this project. I thank her for that trust and for her unstinting willingness to put in the time to make it right.

I am grateful also to Julie's colleagues and other artists who contributed recollections or commentaries—including Herbert Blau, I Nyoman Catra, Elliot Goldenthal, Jeffrey Horowitz, Norman Lear, Jessye Norman, Seiji Ozawa, Stephen Sondheim, and Robert Stattel. Hildred Geertz, Julius Novick, Rajika Puri, and Wendy Gimbel read the manuscript and offered helpful feedback. At Abrams, Diana Murphy's fine critical cyc, openness, and sense of shared adventure not only made a substantive contribution to the final product, but made the editing process a pleasure.

Finally, my thanks to the Rutgers University Research Council, to Dean Marilyn Somville of the Mason Gross School of the Arts, and Theater Arts Chair Bill Esper for support that facilitated my undertaking this exciting venture.

Eileen Blumenthal

Francis, a minister of the court, in Fool's Fire.

INDEX

Julie Taymor with characters from Fool's Fire.

Music Theater Group (New York), 31
Mutius (in *Titus Andronicus*), *188*

N

Nanda (in *Transposed Heads*), 26, *105*, 106–9, *106*, *109*, *111*
National Geographic, 82
Neals, Lawrence A., Jr., *137*, *138*
Neihardt, John, 79
Nelson, Richard, 131
New York Newsday, 38
New York Post, 36
New York Shakespeare Festival/Public Theater (New York), 21, 71
New York Times, 33, 35, 36, 38, 51
New York University, 45
Noh theater, Japanese, 17, 41, 86
Norman, Jessye, 8, 39, *39*, 41, 52, *158*
Novick, Julius, 38

O

Oberlin College, 10–13, 45
O'Connell, Patrick, *50*
Oditz, Carol, 95, 105
Odyssey, The (Homer), 21
Oedipus Rex (Stravinsky/Cocteau), 8, 38–43, *38*, *39*, *40*, 51, 158–69, *158*, *160*, *162*, *165*, *167*, *168*, 186
Okada, Kimi, 30, 95
Okun, Alexander, 27, 105, 109
Orent, Kerry, 144
Ovid, 187
Ozawa, Seiji, 8, 38, *38*, *40*, 41, 158

P

Pamina (in *Magic Flute*), *42*, 171, 173, *173*, *174*, *177*, *178*
Pantalone (in *King Stag*), *92*
Papageno (in *Tempest*), 43
Papp, Joseph, 21, 71
Pappagena (in *Magic Flute*), *177*, 178
Pappageno (in *Magic Flute*), *172*, 173, *174*, *177*, 178, *178*
Parsons, David, 144
Passover Seder, 71. *See also Haggadah, The*
PBS, 50, 51, 71, 115, 144, 158
Peer Gynt (Ibsen), 13
"Penny Arcade Nightmares" (PANs), 187–200, *188*, *190*, *191*
Peter Schumann's Bread and Puppet Theater (New York), 11, 21
Petit, Leonard, 32, *132*, *133*
Petruchio (in *Taming of the Shrew*), 127–28, *127*
Pharaoh's sorcerers (in *Haggadah*), *71*
Phippin, Jackson, 21, 23, 80
Play (Boerwinkel), 13
Playwright's Lab of Sundance Institute, 24
Poe, Edgar Allan, 9, 45, 50, 144
Poernomo, Hadi, 18, 19–20
Pompidou, Dr. (in *Liberty's Taken*), *30*, 103
Porter, Andrew, 43
Prince, Harold, 7, 33, *33*, 52
Prospero (in *Tempest*), 34, 35, 115–23, *115*, *117*, *118*, *121*, *123*, *124*

puppetry, puppet-making:
  as act of devotion, 16–17
  in *Black Elk Lives*, 79
  Bunraku, 17, 88, 123, 133–36
  in *Fool's Fire*, 146, *152*
  in *Grendel*, 44
  in *Juan Darién*, 33, 131, 133–36, *135*, *138*
  in *King Stag*, 86–87
  kite concept and, 86
  in *Liberty's Taken*, "light," 22, 23–24, 44, 86–88
  in *Magic Flute*, 42
  pre-Bunraku, 13
  in psychodrama, 21
  shadow. *See* shadow puppetry
  in *Tempest*, 123
  in *Way of Snow*, 15, *15*
Puri, Rajika, 105, *105*, 106

Q

Queen of the Night (in *Magic Flute*), 173, *173*, *174*, *177*, *181*
Quiroga, Horacio, 31, 131

R

rabbis (in *Haggadah*), *75*
Rabelais, François, 50
Ran (film), 41
Rape of the Sabine Women, 37, 183
Rashomon (film), 22
Rendra, W. S., 13–14, 26
Requiem Mass. *See "Juan Darién"*
Robert Kalfin's Chelsea Theater Company (New York), 11
Roché, Sebastian, *188*
Roland, 15–17, *18*
Romulus and Remus, *183*
Rudko, Michael, *195*

S

St. Clement's Church (New York), 33, 37, 131
Saito Kinen Festival (Japan), 38, *38*, 158
Salome (Strauss), 43
Sappington, Margo, 105
Sarastro (in *Magic Flute*), *42*, 171, *172*, 173, *178*
Saunders, Dan, *40*
Savages (Hampton), 7, 23–24, *23*, 32, 80–83, *80*, *82*, 86
Schikaneder, Emanuel, 171
schoolteacher (in *Juan Darién*), 32–33, *32*, *132*, 133
sculpture, Cycladic, 158, 160, *167*
Sedna (in *Way of Snow*), 55, *60*
Seeds of Atreus, The (Oberlin Group), 12
Serban, Andrei, 20, 24, 85
Sergel, Christopher, 79
Serpent, The (Joseph Chaikin's Open Theater), 10
shadow puppetry, 9, 13, 22
  elusiveness and mystery of, 79
  farces, 32–33
  in *Haggadah*, *75*, *76*
  in *Juan Darién*, 33, 131, 133–36, *135*, *138*
  in *Liberty's Taken*, *103*

  in "Tiger Tales" interludes, 33, 131, *138*
  wayang kulit, 13
  in *Way of Snow*, *58*
Shakespeare, William, 13, 22, 33–38, 115, 118, 127, 183. *See also "Taming of the Shrew, The"; "Tempest, The"; "Titus Andronicus"*
Shakespeare Festival Theater (Stratford, Conn.), 35, 115
Shiraishi, Kayoko, 51
Shiridaman (in *Transposed Heads*), 26, *105*, 106–9, *106*, *111*, *113*
Sinisiri, Duke and Duchess of (in *Fool's Fire*), *148*
Sita (in *Tirai*), *69*
Sita (in *Transposed Heads*), 106, *109*, *111*, *113*
Situmorang, Sitor, 17
Skannal, Lesley, 80
Slawbunk, Desire (in *Liberty's Taken*), 98, *101*
Smeraldina (in *King Stag*), 25, *25*
Smith, Louise, *115*
Smith, Priscilla, 20
Smithsonian Institution, 22
Solomon, Alisa, 27
Sondheim, Stephen, 33
Sophocles, 158
Speaker (in *Magic Flute*), *172*
Stattel, Robert, 34, *36*, 37, *115*
Stein, Adam, *188*
Stephano (in *Tempest*), *121*, 122
Stewart, Ellen, 20
Straiges, Tony, 80
Stravinsky, Igor, 8, 158–60
Sturges, Glenn, *154*
Suarti, *69*
Suehsdorf, David, 27, *28*, 30, 95
Suharno, 60
Sumandhi, I Nyoman, *69*
Sundance Film Festival (Park City, Utah), 45, 144, 158
Swados, Elizabeth, 21, 71

T

Talking Band, 22
Taman Ismail Marzuki (TIM), 13, 15
Taming of the Shrew, The (adaptation of Shakespeare), 13, 35–36, 126–29, *127*, *128*
Tamino (in *Magic Flute*), *42*, 171, 172–73, *178*
Tamora (in *Titus Andronicus*), 187–90, *191*, *193*, 198
Tanaka, Min, 39–41, *160*
Tartaglia (in *King Stag*), 85, *85*, 86, *86*, *89*, *91*, *92*
Taymor, Julie:
  avant-garde training of, 10–12
  awards received, 11–12, 33, *33*, 41, 43, 51, 52
  childhood and high-school years of, 10, *10*
  college education of, 11
  in Denpasar, 16–17
  design work and psychodrama of, 21–26
  directing original adaptations, 26–33
    See also specific works
  in India and Sri Lanka, 10

PHOTOGRAPH CREDITS